I0637288

ANYWHERE ELSE

University Press of Florida

Florida A&M University, Tallahassee
Florida Atlantic University, Boca Raton
Florida Gulf Coast University, Ft. Myers
Florida International University, Miami
Florida State University, Tallahassee
New College of Florida, Sarasota
University of Central Florida, Orlando
University of Florida, Gainesville
University of North Florida, Jacksonville
University of South Florida, Tampa
University of West Florida, Pensacola

rachel knox

anywhere else

ESSAYS ON FLORIDA

University Press of Florida

Gainesville / Tallahassee / Tampa / Boca Raton

Pensacola / Orlando / Miami / Jacksonville / Ft. Myers / Sarasota

Cover image: creacart / istockphoto

Cover and text design: Mindy Basinger Hill

Published in the United States of America

Designed and composed in Adobe Aldine by Mindy Basinger Hill

31 30 29 28 27 26   6 5 4 3 2 1

A record of cataloging-in-publication information is available
from the Library of Congress.

ISBN 978-0-8130-8151-9

The University Press of Florida is the scholarly publishing agency for the
State University System of Florida, comprising Florida A&M University,
Florida Atlantic University, Florida Gulf Coast University, Florida
International University, Florida State University, New College of Florida,
University of Central Florida, University of Florida, University of North
Florida, University of South Florida, and University of West Florida.

University Press of Florida
2046 NE Waldo Road
Suite 2100
Gainesville, FL 32609
floridapress.org

GPSR EU Authorized Representative: Mare Nostrum Group B.V., Maurits-
kade 21D, 1091 GC Amsterdam, The Netherlands, gpsr@mare-nostrum.co.uk

FOR ADAM,

FOREVER AND EVER

contents

author's note

The book you are about to read contains material that may be sensitive to some people. The essays explore themes of violence, murder, sexual assault, addiction, and other heavy subjects. I know firsthand the indelible marks these experiences can leave on a person, and I hope you will read this book with an open heart and self-preservation in mind. Some names and identifying features have been changed to protect anonymity.

ANYWHERE ELSE

introduction / let us alone

In high school, I had friends who worked on St. Pete Beach, clip-ping sunburnt Midwesterners into harnesses and driving the parasail boats that lifted them out of the sparkling Gulf of Mexico into the sky. A yellow parachute with a giant smiley face emblazoned on its back drifted behind them while these workers, mostly teenage boys, steered them across the ocean and brought them down safely into the bathtub-warm water with barely a splash. Those kids had grown up on the water and could drive those boats with their eyes closed. Sometimes the tourists were nice, throwing twenties their way after a day of drinking rum punches at the hotel bar. Most of the time, though, they were dismissive at best, hostile at worst, treating the kids who held their risk of body injury at bay with little regard. We all talked about tourists with a bad attitude, even though they were the sole providers of our minimum-wage jobs at seafood restaurants, ice cream shops, mini-golf courses, and the parasail boats.

To make some extra money on the side, the boys started screen-printing T-shirts they'd sell at parties and in the parking lots of local hardcore shows, their target market being other locals and beach-rat kids. The most popular shirt they made sported a simple but effective message: *YOU FLEW HERE, I GREW HERE* in bold text above and below the silhouette of a pelican, the same logo that graces the manholes, flags, and tourism ads for our city of St. Pete.

St. Pete had its fair share of retirees when I was growing up, sure, but it was nothing like it is now, a tidal wave of Midwestern transplants crowding into the luxury condos that have popped up on every square inch of available space like crabgrass. Growing up, my friends and neighbors were almost all third-, fourth-, and fifth-generation Floridians. Their parents or grandparents had come here in the fifties, sold a promise of eternal sunshine and cheap housing, smelled the confederate jasmine blooming on every corner, and never left.

My friends and I called it "the vortex": the strong gravitational orbit that kept so many people we knew stuck in place. They might move out of their parents' houses, but not the city limits, never venturing further north than to spend a few years in Gainesville or Tallahassee for college. Inevitably, with few exceptions, they came back. We would see them out sometimes, skulking around our local dive bar with an edgy air about them, nursing a PBR and talking about how much it still sucked here. Eventually, I set my sights on total escape, somewhere far enough away that I could break the vortex's pull and reinvent myself. Of course, I was grateful for the obvious things: almost year-round sunshine; my secret beach spot, nestled behind a copse of mangroves; fried grouper sandwiches and afternoons whiled away inside the musty walls of Haslam's.

But Florida's population has exploded, especially after the pandemic. Roughly a thousand people move here every day, most of them in their early twenties, working remote jobs or living a "digital nomad" lifestyle. They're drawn here by the promise of a slower pace, stellar beaches, and a chance to cosplay the "Salt Life" persona without actually *becoming* Floridians. Their out-of-state license plates tell on them, as does their skittish driving in our frequent tropical rainstorms. They fill our hometown sports stadiums in their Orioles and Yankee jerseys and keep their blue-state voter registrations intact. When I was of the age most of the transplants that I battle with for beach parking are now, I couldn't *wait* to leave. I dreamed of the moment I finally had enough money saved to get the hell out of St. Pete and see the rest of the world.

Eventually, I did just that. I sold my car, my records, and everything I owned and moved to New York City in 2013. It was there, in a dim Brooklyn bar, that a new friend, upon hearing I had come from Florida a few years prior, made a joke. I can't remember exactly what the friend said now, but I'm sure you could speculate. You know it, right? Something about people eating bath salts, about alligators or trailer parks. A reference to Casey Anthony or the Cocaine Cowboys or Elián González or some other story ripped from the past two decades of headlines, stripped of any context. But you know, don't you, that the sentence had the tenor of a joke.

No one hears that you're from Florida and says in response, "Oooooh, *lucky!*" Your Florida provenance becomes your defining characteristic. Their eyes widen, or they chuckle, or they launch into a series of questions that are both nonsensical and revealing of the wide gulf between their understanding of the state and your own experience living there. I mean, sure, I couldn't wait to leave, but it wasn't *that* bad, was it?

When my new friend made the dig, I felt my cheeks burn, a familiar mixture of anger and embarrassment roiling in my stomach. I saw myself reflected in their eyes—no longer a sophisticate, but a different kind of creature: a tramp-stamped beach rat, crazed and barefoot in a 7-Eleven. A meme. And I guess I sort of *was* that creature, to be honest with you—I *have* been barefoot in a 7-Eleven. In my defense, I was five and had fire-ant bites from running in the grass, but it still stung to be perceived that way. It pissed me off. How would they know anything about my life in Florida? That joke was only funny when I made it.

After she left, I found myself thinking: *How did this happen? When did Florida become such a joke to Americans from the rest of the country?* Florida's identity in the national imagination had become a caricature when I wasn't looking. Like my friends who made those T-shirts, I'd always been proud of my locals-only status, a person born and raised in a place with so many temporary and transient residents. It was only when I left Florida to live in New York City that I realized the people who fly there every winter sure have a lot of mean things to say about us behind our backs.

So what do you think of when you picture a Floridian? What do they look like? What are they wearing? What do they do for a living, have for dinner? If you imagine a day in their life, what does it look like? If your answer contained two or more punchlines, you're probably in the majority. You're probably also not from Florida. It's easy to make the jokes because we've been fed a constant stream of them for the last ten years or so, as bizarre headlines and news stories found traction in the "clickbait" era of the early aughts, spurred on by sites like Cracked, BuzzFeed, and the like. If you're from Florida and the jokes still automatically came to mind, I get it; I was also, however briefly, a self-loathing Floridian.

One of my favorite Floridians once wrote a song blaming a woman, but when it comes to Florida, I have to disagree with Jimmy, for the most part. This change in the cultural tide is arguably driven by white dudes: Jeb Bush, George Zimmerman, Joe Exotic (of *Tiger King* fame), and the ubiquitous "Florida Man" I'd grown so tired of hearing about. Politicians and public figures are what people see and how they form opinions about a place they've never been. I think that's only natural, but these men aren't the whole story. They aren't even the first chapter.

In the past decade, I've grown defensive of a place I hadn't known I cared so much about. As I pontificated to strangers in bars and new friends with a fervor that surprised me, I realized something. I loved Florida, deeply, and maybe always had. My teenage longing to leave felt more like what it actually was: teenage longing, something everyone probably feels. It was less about the place I was from and more about the person I wanted to be. Something had told me I couldn't be that person in Florida, but I was finally starting to disbelieve it.

The whole time I lived in New York, I missed Florida dearly—wanted to brag about it, to show others its good side, to describe the way the sky looks during one of our million-dollar sunsets. I wanted to make everyone who chuckled sit down at the edge of a dock, eat a Cuban sandwich, and wash it down with a cold beer or Rum Runner. I wanted to walk with them through a silent pine forest in the early morning, looking for scrub jays. I wanted to take them mudding, to the rodeo, to the fish fry on the corner, the lighthouses dotting the coasts. Down the cobblestone streets of St. Augustine, America's oldest city, where a gust of salt air and a squint of the eyes might make you believe you're in Seville five hundred years ago. To steer them down Crystal River in the spring, when the manatees swarm and bump up against your kayak with whiskered noses. And then challenge them: try to tell me, now, that this place is a joke.

I realized that writing into those feelings might be more effective than starting bar fights about them. I was already writing about Florida all the time anyway, even when I tried not to. It came bubbling up whenever I tried to make sense, on the page, of the events of my girlhood and the person I became as a result. The heat and sweat and buzzing of cicadas bled into every scene, prompting comments from the other students in my writing classes about how I seemed "really obsessed with *place*." I started looking for any depiction of Florida that went against the narrative I kept hearing in order to hold them up to my own life, looking for gaps, and this book was born.

I went down the rabbit hole of the movies and stories I'd grown up watching, those that had shaped my growing identity: *Wild Things,* with its swampy, steamy teenage criminals; Aileen Wuornos, whose trial and execution I remembered seeping into the early years of my life, but hadn't realized was so close to my own circumstances until the Hollywood version, *Monster,* won Oscars. On the way, other things kept putting themselves into my inquiring path, like art I'd never known was connected to Florida or had been too young to fully understand. A subconscious dislike for the Thomas Kinkade paintings I saw everywhere in my religious community led me to consider the complicated history of The Highwaymen, a collective of African American landscape painters whose work depicting Florida is still under-celebrated for all the reasons you might imagine. Florida's history, in art and in reality, has always been messy.

It's the people who make Florida both messy and majestic, just like they do anywhere else. I'm sure there's a "Wisconsin Man"; we just don't know about him. But I do know about Floridians. I thought about them a lot while I was writing this book. They're the ones I picture when I ask myself the question I asked you earlier: what does a *real* Floridian look like? I thought about them while driving around my hometown after moving back, watching all my favorite bars close and high-rise condos stretch precariously toward the sky. As comedians joked about us on late-night shows while another wave of red tide bloomed along the Gulf and our manatee population dwindled, I pictured their faces. *I bet that guy has a vacation home on Longboat Key,* I said to them in my head, as the studio audience applauded the host's punchline about meth heads while he grinned into his coffee mug. *Leave us alone,* I thought, *stop coming here in droves while constantly talking about how much you hate us.*

I pictured people like my childhood best friend's mom, a fifth-generation Floridian and one of the few deep-sea fisherwomen to cut a wake in the Gulf. She took us lobstering and scalloping, even sometimes shark fishing in the middle of the night. She showed us how to chum the waters, spot ripples on the surface, and safely get the hell out of the way while she brought a dinosaur on board. Her hands never shook while she handled and measured it, showed us its panting gills, and released it back into the inky black. I pictured Ms. Gwen—who you had better call Ms. Gwendolyn Reese until she tells you otherwise—the legendary community leader, CEO, and president of the African American Heritage Association of St. Petersburg. She's spent decades fighting for a future that benefits all Floridians in the face of mass corporate development, displacement, and gentrification. In between the countless hours of work she's done for the residents of the city, she has also managed to outdress every last one of them.

I pictured my friend Mark, who was in a biker gang when we were kids but now walks the line, mostly. In his punk-country band, he plays songs about swamp outlaws that send waves of goosebumps down my arms, a pastiche of Florida past and present, a conjuring of all the ghosts of friends and cowboys that sometimes still feel like they're there with us, wafting around with the smoke in a dark dive bar in Myakka. I think about Charlotte, who helps run a Facebook group devoted to campsite trading at our state parks. The group is open only to year-round Florida residents, a little grassroots army against the bots and venture-funded apps that try to snap the sites up and sell them to tourists for major holidays. Charlotte and her family know all of the secrets: the hidden springs, the quiet trails, the best place to find shark's teeth and fossils and really good barbeque. I think of all of those friends—the poets and singers and activists and booksellers and bartenders—and none of them are a punchline. They share one important quality: they love this place, in all of its messiness, wrongness, and wildness. I wrote this book for them, and for you.

By telling my own stories, I wanted to shout over the people who aren't from here. So often, they are the ones who get to write about us—the headlines, the think pieces, the national op-eds. Why should pundits and politicians and people who have only ever been to Miami on spring break get to tell us what it's like to live here? Why should all of the discussion about Florida happen without actual Floridians at the table? If being a lifelong reader has taught me anything, it's that the main function of books is to change your mind. That's why powerful people are so keen on banning them, isn't it? Because one person writing about their life can upend everything you thought you knew. More voices joining a chorus only adds to the beauty of its harmonies; more colors in a palette deepen and complicate the contours of a painting.

It can sometimes feel very selfish or narcissistic to write about oneself, to imagine that anyone would care about the particulars of your individual experience. But I hope that by reading this book, in seeing Florida through my eyes and the art that tries (and sometimes fails!) to tell a more nuanced story about this place, you might think more deeply about your perception of this place.

Maybe you'll never stop making fun of us, even as you visit on vacation, even as we are imperiled and abandoned and reviled but never let alone. Maybe, after hearing about my life, you will feel even *more* strongly that Floridians are nuts. But maybe you will leave with a little more empathy, with a better understanding of *why* we are so devoted to this hot, messy, deeply flawed, and desperately beautiful patch of sandy swamp jutting into the ocean. All we want is to be free, wild, and maybe, yes, a little trashy. To love what we love the same way you do, even if it makes no sense to you. It isn't *for* you. It's for us. Believe me, we get the joke. We just don't want to be one anymore. Listen to our stories, take us seriously, afford us the same agency and dignity as anyone else, and please, stop feeding the goddamn seagulls.

wild things

Imagine: The girl from the trailer park doesn't die at the end. She sails away with all the money.

"You're dead!" Kevin Bacon yells.

"No, I'm not," says Neve Campbell, loading a harpoon into her shotgun.

In this story, 1998's *Wild Things,* the teenage girl from this Everglades trailer park is named Suzie. She's been, at turns, victim and then villain; she's changed her story so many times across the last two hours of screen time that it's hard for both of us, character and viewer, to remember which one she really is.

Right now, she's on a sailboat. There are two men on the boat with her: Detective Ray Duquette, played by Bacon; and her high-school-guidance-counselor-turned-accomplice-turned-lover Sam Lombardo, played by a slightly too-convincing Matt Dillon. Suzie dispenses first with Bacon (harpoon to the gut) and then with the duplicitous Dillon. With her former lover, she employs her feminine wiles and a little liquid poison. She delivers a cheery monologue about multiple-choice tests and Medea as he coughs and sputters. The speech is really, I think, about the obtuseness of male treachery. (So obvious, so telegraphed, so unlike the slow-churning whirlpool that is the wrath of a woman scorned.) Then, while Dillon's grabbing at his throat and staggering around the deck of the boat, she undoes the winch and releases the sail with purpose, knocking him ass-over-teakettle into the wide, green Gulf.

Our hero, though she is a teenage girl, is not carried off on horseback into the sunset. She sits behind no clinking suit of armor, no big boy hands guiding the reins. Richard Gere, in his starched-white collar, does not stride into the factory to scoop her into the crook of his arms and carry her out to applause.

Instead, our hero is alone. She has a bad blonde wig, a yellow one-piece bathing suit, and her entire future spooling out ahead of her. She is finally, blissfully, free.

The story I want to tell is, like Suzie's, confusing. Twisted. Winding. It's a python, curving itself around a cypress knee in murky water. It occurs to me that maybe the truth actually contains many diametrically opposed truths within itself, an ouroboros of meaning, the python eating itself.

～

Emma told me, "I think it's important that you don't decide on a term for it. You don't want to, like, muzzle it before you even write it. Just see what happens."

We were at the beach, squinting out at the Gulf of Mexico from cheap plastic chairs. We were talking about writing, about a someday-book I imagine writing. I told her that I felt a little manic, like the writing was a live wire I was trying to grab onto. It might be too raw.

If I let myself think too long about what I was really trying to say, I started to feel charged. Ionically, I mean. Like particles were bouncing around inside of me, and if I didn't rub my feet on some neutral surface, I'd get shocked when I tried to touch it. I was trying not to be dramatic. I was not ignoring it out of fear or shame, I don't think. I just didn't have the language yet.

Something was happening, though.

Emma left, kissing the top of my head goodbye and warning me to reapply my sunscreen. I was lost in thought and stayed for a long time, searching for something in the pages of the book I was reading that would snap all of my disconnected thoughts into place, like iron shavings racing toward some giant, existential magnet.

I got horribly sunburnt, ankle to kneecap to ass cheek to elbow. I burned cleanly down the middle, left side on fire where the sun beat down from the west. When I got to a mirror, I had to laugh at the sight of my naked body, all lopsided triangles and shocking white sections of negative space. I was a little ashamed. I'm from Florida; sunburns weren't supposed to happen to me. I knew better.

We used to have this joke—my high school friends Autumn and Audrey and I. It was less of a joke, I guess, and more of a persona we would try on: the succubus. It's an old myth, but it felt new to us, however we encountered it (I can't remember). We were in high school, and we were all three reading a lot of dark shit at the time. Sylvia Plath. *Twilight. Maxim.*

A mythical creature who descends upon men in dreams, the succubus overwhelms them, against their protestation. She gains her life force by stealing something carnal from their incapacitated bodies. Whenever we did something wild outside the bounds of our normal standards, fueled either by alcohol or the egging on of the other two, we blamed it on the succubus. We pretended we'd turned into her, gnashing our teeth, undulating our hips, laughing. I'd text Audrey the morning after we went out, tapping my nails on my Nokia's T9 keys:

> Me: *sry. went 2 eric's and passed out. wut happened w/ polo shirt guy you were talking 2?*
>
> Audrey: *succubus came out ;) he called me 3x today so far.*

We tried on the succubus persona like a disguise, seeing how far we could take it. I once watched a fifteen-year-old Autumn convince grown men to let her take their five-figure motorcycles for a spin around the block. This, despite her lack of a driver's license and the presence of her giant heels, too big for her feet. Child's play. She had dimples.

The power of a young woman is enormous. Soul-sucking. Makes you woozy. It is also flimsy, ephemeral, not real.

~

I didn't grow up in a trailer park like Suzie, nor did I even live in one myself for any significant period of time. But I spent a lot of time in trailers. My grandparents lived in one, and I spent every summer there until I was "too old." I loved it there—loved the bounce of the floor when I ran from one end to the other; loved the iron vents on the floorboards, where I could see through to the red-clay dirt underneath; loved the clock on the wall that played a different bird call at the top of each hour.

Many years later, as an adult, my childhood friend Devo visited me while on vacation. I was back in St. Pete after a decade away in New York. When we first met, Devo lived in a trailer. Now, we were grownups, a wonder; she was a flight attendant, her little blue location dot on "Find My Friends" always somewhere new and exotic when I checked on her. She brought me perfume, strawberry candy, and fancy lotion from Berlin.

When we have drinks at a beach bar, we start talking about all our old friends. She and I weren't as close as the rest of the girls we knew; it took us until adulthood to catch up. I always attributed this to my semi-outsider status, the fact that they all lived in Sarasota, and I lived an hour's drive over the Sunshine Skyway Bridge, mostly driving down for hardcore shows without my parents' knowledge. She mentioned in passing that none of our other friends had been inside her mobile home. I had, only a few weeks after meeting her for the first time. This surprised me.

"But you were so much better friends with the others," I told her. "Why me?"

"They all had money, though," she said with a shrug. "I guess I knew you wouldn't judge me."

She didn't mean it as an insult, but even if she did, I wouldn't care. She laughed the wicked laugh that I love, cocked her head to the side, and sipped her margarita. She put her hand on mine, and we gossiped some more.

After she flew back to Knoxville, I wandered around my house like a hungry ghost. I felt something weaving itself between us, retroactively, something that had always been there that I couldn't name.

I've been thinking about this old saying: "There are three sides to every story: your side, their side, and the truth." People only seem to say this, I've noticed, when both parties are lying.

One of the reasons I love *Wild Things* is because it never decides who is telling the truth. Everyone is lying. People cross and double-cross one another, to almost comedic effect. They swear they are telling the truth, then a judge bangs a gavel. In the next shot, they come out from lurking around a corner and call their enemy "partner" with a knowing smile.

"Ken, I am not fucking my students," says Matt Dillon, a guidance counselor who is actively fucking his students. There are five sides to this story, each holding a gun at one another, an endless standoff.

~

When I was a younger woman—nineteen, twenty, twenty-one—I mostly used my she-powers for good. I loved my bartending job at Sloppy Pelican, a greasy spoon at the north end of the beach. I lured hefty tips out of the salty dogs who wasted their social security checks on pitchers of Coors Light and grouper sandwiches.

They were easily beguiled by my mastery of that most ancient, most girlish state of being: captivity. I spent hours propped up on one elbow, listening to their stories, smiling and nodding. We had a lot of the same interests, actually: Raymond Chandler, the slow decline in the quality of service at our local Waffle House, crossword puzzles. They brought me old news clippings and photographs of themselves next to surfboards, somewhere in the Pacific Theater, leis dangling around their sepia-toned erstwhile hardbodies. I always started the shift with a twenty-dollar bill in the jukebox, playing my favorite doo-wop songs.

Sometimes their eyes would grow misty, telling me I reminded them of their daughters. Sometimes their eyes went flinty and hard, and they told me I could get a man in a lot of trouble. I wondered whose daughters they were thinking of then.

The learned defensiveness would set in—too many beers and my most beloved regular would cop a feel, moon-faced, starry-eyed. I'd swat wandering hands away and wonder if I was being a bitch. *He doesn't know what he's doing, right?*

I'd take their cash and immediately redistribute it after my shifts, visiting my fellow industry friends at their own beach bar shifts. I was usually off by happy hour, and before I biked home to my downtown apartment, I would ride down the beach, stopping to say hi to the girls. I drank "007s"—Stoli Orange, fresh-squeezed Florida orange juice, and 7UP—and left fistfuls of cash in my wake. On their own days off, they would curl their hair, come to my bar for happy hour before their night shifts, and repeat the cycle. We were mermaids in tank tops and Air Force 1s, separating men from their money clean as a bowline. Those days, I felt bronzed and invincible.

These days, my hair still has a physical reaction to being on the seashore, caked in dried saltwater. It curls and piles up like a sentient thing, a sculptural mass that looks best with the arms of sunglasses stabbed into its tangled nest. The soles of my feet stay sand-burnt and calloused against molten asphalt, even after a decade away; I can flamingo-hop from sidewalk to floorboard with the best of them. I go to beach bars wherever I am, looking for some signposts from my girlhood. I speak the lingua franca that demarcates me as one of their own: "Beerandashot, please."

I wonder if my patina is showing. I imagine how I'd look cast in bronze, shoulders back, immobilized, no legs to speak of, bound and beautiful on the bow of some great ship.

Thinking like this wears me out. It's emotional time travel. Sometimes the scenes come back in the wrong order.

"You're doing shadow work," Emma had said before at the beach. "I could cry if I think about it for too long. You're talking to little Rachel."

At the time, Emma was a licensed therapist, employed as a high school guidance counselor, like Sam Lombardo. (She was not fucking her students.) She had promised never to "therapize me" when we were together, but secretly, I loved that she couldn't help it. I liked being therapized.

I liked that idea too—shadow work. It sounded like I was practicing witchcraft. Or I was battling to the death with my teenage self, *Mortal Kombat*-style, her hands shooting out dark clouds at my grown-up face. I imagined sweeping her shiny, young leg with my creaky, present-day limbs, pictured me boxing her little ears, admonishing her. *How could you be so stupid?*

Other times, I saw myself gently taking the harsh Noxzema pads out of teenage Rachel's hands and throwing them in the garbage. Putting in her retainer before she went to bed so her teeth might not end up as crooked as they did. I imagined brushing, and then braiding, her constantly tangled hair.

I read some statistic once about how victims of sexual assault were several times more likely than others to suffer from chronic pain: debilitating migraines, backaches, suppressed immune systems.

What an added insult, I remember thinking at the time, sitting at my kitchen table, a dumb mask of concern on my face. *That sucks so much.*

For those *people.*

Sitting in my beach chair, the tide rushed up to my burning toes, cooling them for a second. A dark tide crept up inside my slow-cooking mind.

~

The sheer volume of wildlife in Florida is unsettling. Everywhere I go, there are creatures. I made a list on my phone's Notes app, and in just one day, I saw wild peacocks on Park Street, escaped from the rich people's houses; feral parrots in Gulfport; a flock of ibis bobbing for worms in the empty lot behind Lynn Blue Crab; a heron can-can-stepping in the middle of Fifty-Eighth Street while traffic waits patiently; dozens of lizards; box turtles; a giant dead wasp in a patio chair at my mom's; two crows scrounging for dropped fries at Woody's Waterfront; and three dolphins while I wait for a car to surrender its metered spot on Pass-a-Grille.

Birds everywhere: skimmers, pelicans, plovers, egrets, stilts. I went to the beach and, while I was distracted by my book, a seagull, still in midair, deep-throated the pork rind I was attempting to put into my mouth, halfway through its journey, and flew away with his prize before I could process what just happened. Inland, I encountered sandhill cranes at inopportune times—walking across a Walmart parking lot, looking absentmindedly at my phone—when one was suddenly in my path, all glittery-eyed and prehistoric. Being here makes me jumpy. Around every corner, there is something coiled, waiting to strike if I step on it.

Whenever I bring up *Wild Things*, eyes light up. It's almost a guarantee that the first thing the person I am talking to will remember is That Scene. When I was a teenager, boys spoke about it in giddy whispers. Neve Campbell and Denise Richards in a pool, kissing, while Sam

Lombardo watches. All three of them in the motel room afterward, the first threesome any of us can remember. Those same boys, now men at parties or bars, recall the scene with reverence when the film is brought up, no doubt having attached their own formative memories to what accounts for maybe one and a half minutes of screen time in a full-length movie.

It's a shame that this is what people think of when you mention *Wild Things*. Of course, though, that's what people remember. I wonder if the filmmakers knew that would be all anyone talked about, if that's why they put it in all the trailers. Was it an intentional choice, guaranteed to bring horny viewers to theaters? Or was it just one of those things, played for laughs at first, that grew and grew until it swallowed up a whole story?

"The story is actually good," I always try to tell people, "if you would just watch it. Neo-noir. Really clever writing." But the person across from me isn't listening anymore. Bikini tops are being untied in the film reels of their minds.

～

Sometimes I wonder if I am hot. Okay, often.

Okay, all the time.

I think that's probably normal. Hot is complicated. But you know it when you see it. It's not the same as beautiful, which carries with it some sense of artistic integrity, some timelessness, some preservation. Women don't get to be dignified in old age like men do. *Stately,* they're called. *Grand dames* if they've aged relatively well; *crones, hags,* or *biddies* if they haven't. Old ladies aren't hot, unless they're being fetishized. But given these options, I still find myself reluctant to be fearful of the process of aging in the way that I am probably supposed to. I don't think it's that scary to grow old, given the alternative.

I have watched too many of the young women I knew, when I was myself a young woman, die before they were supposed to. They left me before I could see how their faces changed, where the wrinkles would have crept in around their laugh lines. I imagine how much salt would pepper into their hair. I find myself wishing I had danced with them more instead of being too worried about my moves, how I looked to men, watching the wilder ones and sipping my drink stoically at the table. I wish I had smothered them, my friends, suffocated them with my love, embarrassed them. I should have draped my arms around their necks like a flag, declared them for what they were, after all: my home country.

I was always so lost in my own thoughts. Too reticent with my expressions of love. *For shame,* I scold myself now.

I think about how, in an alternate universe, I could hold them around their now-stretch-marked hips while we tiptoe across the sand in our bikinis. Their babies would be teeter-tottering, wet fists jammed into their smiling maws, clinging to my calves. I would feed these babies fistfuls of Goldfish and supply their mothers with endless compliments and cans of White Claw. I'd be smiling like an idiot, a person to whom nothing bad had ever happened, and all would be right with the world. The sun would melt like a popsicle into the horizon, bleeding rose gold and burnt sienna all over their freckled, smiling faces.

Getting older, I have realized with each premature funeral I have attended, is an unthinkable, indescribable gift. My emerging wrinkles are thumbprints on a much-handled face, proof that I have made it this far, that people have touched me, kissed me, and made me laugh over and over again. Getting old is pure, dumb, stupid fucking luck.

It is also proof that I am, so far, invincible. Unkillable.

The subtle sag of the collagen in my cheeks, the creaks and pops I hear when I propel myself out of bed in the morning. My propensity toward comfort, toward soft clothes and strong drinks and a quiet life. They are a middle finger to all of the things and people that have wanted me dead.

So it's not with anxiety that I am searching for something in my reflection. It's with curiosity. I'm just not sure where she went, that little Rachel. I see her sometimes, in quick glimpses. In a bar bathroom, when I'm snapping a leotard between my thighs, thinking about how many leotards I stole from American Apparel. When someone I went to high school with is there, in the freezer section at Publix—one of the boys whose red face is burned into my memory, him calling me a slut—buying gluten-free Margherita pizzas, and rage comes over me again like a demon possession. I have the urge to run into them, full speed, with my cart, screaming like a banshee.

When it happens, this glimpsing of past me, I have to blink slowly and make sure I am still in the correct corner of the multiverse. I'm not sixteen anymore, thank God. I breathe in, then out, then quietly wheel my shopping cart back toward reality.

~

There was this girl, Hannah. I didn't like Hannah when we were younger. She was mouthy and beautiful in a mean-pixie way, and she was known for talking behind people's backs and making scenes at shows and parties. If you fought back, though—if you told Hannah to say something to your face, if you found her whispering behind an X-stamped hand in a venue bathroom—she'd dissolve into a puddle of crocodile tears. You'd relent, sensing a weaker creature. The next morning, you'd wake up to find a list of everyone you'd hooked up with plastered across the internet like a scarlet letter, or worse. She must have been single-handedly responsible for the distribution of hundreds of nude photographs, boys and girls alike. She was good at the internet, and she didn't play fair. It drove me crazy that she was always, eventually, forgiven by the other girls. I kept her at arm's length, sticking up for myself without crossing her too badly, which made me one of her least favorites but someone she had to be civil with due to our large number of mutual friends.

Which is why my stomach churned, as an adult, when I found myself in the back of a Sprinter van in Tulum, listening to Hannah squeal with laughter as the driver talked in low-voiced Spanglish in the front seat. I was there because our mutual friend Caroline wanted me there, at her bachelorette party. Caroline had warned me on the plane not to be mean to Hannah, knowing full well our mutual dislike of one another. "I'm not the one you need to worry about," I told her. I'd never been a fighter. The other girls we were with had always been the ones to do that for me. Emma had actually fought Hannah before because she had said another friend of ours, who had worn her hair curly to that night's party, looked like a poodle. In that friend's defense, and maybe because she was a little drunk, Emma broke Hannah's face apart. I am not exaggerating. Her jawbone had to be wired back together.

Sitting in the van in Mexico, twelve years after that party, I wondered how well it had healed. Emma had changed her stripes since those days. She'd gone to graduate school and become a licensed de-escalator of physical and mental violence. She had long since stopped beating people up and spoke of that party with a lot of remorse and confusion, hardly recognizing her old self. I hadn't really grown out of my tendency to argue, though, and Hannah had already started to annoy me. Apparently, my sharp tongue was a worse quality than a trigger-happy fist in adulthood. So I kept quiet and looked out the window.

When we arrived at the house we'd rented for the bachelorette weekend, the sun started to slip into the sky, and someone mixed a big batch of margaritas. One by one, we had all gravitated toward the pool and arranged ourselves over deck chairs and daybeds. Emma and I canoodled on the hammock. Hannah reclined with her head near our feet, sunglasses on, one hand saluting over the top of her freckled face like a '40s pinup.

The five of us by the pool had known one another almost our whole lives. Emma and Caroline were born a day apart in the same hospital. Devo and Hannah met the two of them later in middle school. I came into the picture the summer before my freshman year of high school, when I carpooled the hour south to some skatepark show with a few other St. Pete kids. Emma had been sitting in the parking lot, drunk, crying, holding one of her hands. I walked over to her and asked what was wrong. She had a splinter. I had tweezers in my purse, so I dug it out and held her hand until she stopped crying.

As is usually the case when old friends and strong drinks are together, we started talking about the past. We talked about all the boys we'd grown up with—which ones we'd secretly kissed behind one another's backs, who we had run into recently at the gym. We compared our various social media feeds and passed phones around, clucking at the screens and noting who time had treated well and who was, unfortunately, exactly the same. Who we had hated, the exes we remembered fondly. The older boys, who played a game called Not My House, where they showed up at parties and trashed peoples' homes—breaking shit, stealing booze, scrawling slurs on the walls in Sharpie. Several of them are now incarcerated.

One of the boys we'd known back then came up: Elliott. "He has some tiny little girlfriend. She's super young, but I don't think they're married," Devo said. The others swapped stories about him—someone mentioned the horrible skinny jeans he used to wear, basically painted on; another his obsession with anime and whip-its. I suddenly realized that I was speaking, that words were coming out of my mouth. I was recounting, very casually, a time when I'd awoken from a teenage blackout to find Elliott there, in bed next to me. Or not next to, but on top of. For some reason, I was laughing.

Everyone else had gone extremely quiet.

⁓

"Say that again," Devo said, back at the pool, pushing her sunglasses on top of her head.

I wanted to stop there. That is always where I would stop, in my head and on the page. But she made me say it again, what happened to me, and so I could not stop, then or now. I had to keep going, even if it was in circles.

After Devo made me start from the beginning and it all tumbled out, there was silence. Hannah looked at me with an expression I couldn't quite decipher.

"So he raped you," Devo said. I still had to fight the urge to laugh, which was confusing. Something in my brain glitched, and my mouth opened and closed as my signals crossed.

I don't want to write about this. I don't want to think about it. I don't want to admit that, until she said the truth back to me, I did not believe it. Not in the way that I've heard people describe it, where the memory was too painful, or they thought no one would believe them, or they knew they had to stuff it down for survival. Something different, more slippery, is slinking out of my grasp.

⁓

In one of my favorite horror movies, *I Spit on Your Grave,* the heroine is a writer named Jennifer who is trying to get some peace and quiet to finish her novel. She rents a cabin in the woods for solitude but makes the grave mistake of letting some local men perceive her as she stops for gas and groceries on her way to the cabin. They descend on her vacation home and gang-rape her, leaving her for dead. One of the men rips up Jennifer's manuscript, attempting to erase her story. But like Suzie in *Wild Things,* she does not die. She waits. She watches her bruises heal. She tries to put the pieces of her story back together, and then she gets to work.

Systematically, she exacts revenge on each of her attackers, killing them in shockingly graphic ways, each a special, blood-red snowflake of cruelty. She hangs one with a rope, castrates another, uses a boat engine to disembowel one of her attackers while quoting his own cruel words back to him. She kills them in ways that mirror their violations of her, using her writer's imagination to piece her own story back together.

All of the women in these stories, I realize, have weapons. Suzie's harpoon gun in *Wild Things.* Jennifer's rope, a knife, her own sexualized image in *I Spit on Your Grave.*

～

I get a little obsessed with *Wild Things* lore. I pore over trivia about the film's production—the story, the cast on the first day of shooting encountering a dead body floating in the middle of the swamp. Kevin Bacon, reading the script, reportedly saying, "This is the trashiest thing I've ever read. I'm going to produce it." Neve Campbell's strict no-nudity clause; she was still on *Party of Five* at the time and was concerned about this attempt at a crossover, how her fan base would react. Denise Richardson, in her memoir *Real Girl Next Door,* before the famous threesome scene, saying that she and Neve Campbell went to a local bar and downed a pitcher of margaritas.

All of these things mean something to me. They add up to something once I start writing in earnest. This is exactly what I did not want to happen—the story getting away from me.

Denise Richards's first line of dialogue in *Wild Things* is:
"Fuck off."
Matt Dillon's is:
"Settle down."
Neve Campbell's:
"I'm out of here."
It seems to me that these are three distinct courses of action, three things I could tell myself to do. Choose your own adventure.
"Fuck off, Rachel."
"Settle down, Rachel."
"I'm out of here, messy, grasping, incompetent, scatter-brained Rachel."

Emma said, "What's crazy is, if you saw him today and asked him, I guarantee he would say no."

If you're a woman and you have a male partner, imagine asking them, "Have you ever raped someone?"
Do you think they would tell you the truth?

~

Okay. Enough.
I mostly feel nothing about it now. I'm not lying, and I'm not saying that to sound mysterious or aloof. The main thing I notice is an absence of feeling.
Sometimes, I guess, I feel angry. The anger comes out of nowhere when it comes, though, so I can't be sure they're connected. Once, it happened when I was riding my bike on the Pinellas Trail, for no rea-

son, somewhere near where it passes by my high school's football field. I had to pull to the side and sit in the dirt until I could breathe again.

Another time, I went to a plant festival with my mom that I did not realize took place in the community park that was visible from the window of my friend Autumn's house, where it happened. Her bedroom window blinds had cast ribbons of light onto the sheets an hour or so after what happened to me had happened, and I stared and stared and stared at them.

I realized where I was, at the playground, on a swing. The recycled-tire mulch underfoot was the same as the kind I'd kicked up with the toe of my shoe twenty years ago, while I cracked a beer, pushing and pumping my feet, swinging in a jerky figure-eight next to Autumn, in what had to have been another life happening to another person. I was frozen, thinking about all I could have done, what reverse butterfly effect I might have created.

I should have kept pumping my legs, higher and higher. Elliott's hands, my friend's hands, connecting with the small of my back, pushing me as hard as he could. I should have jumped with all my might and taken off running. I should have launched myself straight into the moon.

Instead, in reality, that night, I drank several more beers and fell asleep on Autumn's giant raft of a bed. I woke up to the realization that someone was having sex with me. Or I was having sex with someone. That was strange because only my friends were there. And I did not want to have sex with any of them.

I could tell you that I had some big realization right then, that day at the pool. Some life-changing moment when I said it out loud. That the girls all rallied around me in some kind of *Midsommar* group-shriek. I'd be lying.

The truth is we just kept talking.

"I guess so," I said to Devo's sobering statement. I took another sip of my drink. A brief pause, water lapping at the edge of the pool. Then, someone else started to tell a similar story. Finding themselves in a strange boy's room at a party, not knowing where their friends were. Hazy, snapshot memories of a bathroom stall in some music venue or another. Waking up on a couch with their shirt missing or their jeans unbuttoned. Hannah brought up an old boyfriend, one we'd all adored. She told us that he had regularly threatened to kill himself if she wouldn't sleep with him, that there were times when she woke up after a night out to him, or his hands, inside of her.

I'm trying to get you to see it was no big deal. Right?

~

What our other friends didn't know was that many years earlier, I had called Hannah in a panic.

I was dating an older guy. One morning, I woke up at his house and went to pee. I looked into the trash and remembered, fuzzily, that the condom had broken at some point, but he hadn't stopped.

I realized I probably should take a Plan B. I didn't know where to go to get one. I wasn't on birth control, couldn't even imagine broaching the subject with my strict, Evangelical parents, who I lied to incessantly in order to do what I wanted—usually what my friends were doing. As far as they knew, I'd spent the night at a girlfriend's house down the street, not two counties away. My sister was in college, living her own life, moving on. She was so good, going places. I didn't want her to know what I'd been doing since she left.

So I called Brittany. She was an older punk girl, about twenty, and a friend of the guy I was seeing. She worked at the Planned Parenthood in Sarasota. She was kind and outspoken, impossibly cool, and often passed out Food Not Bombs flyers at shows. She always talked to the younger girls about consent and designated drivers, a den mother in a ripped-up GWAR shirt. She was working that day, luckily, and when I got to the clinic, she helped me through the process of filling out paperwork and brought me the blister pack of medication.

"Do you have somewhere to hang out for a little?" she asked me. "Plan B makes you feel pretty shitty, and you probably won't want to drive back to St. Pete for a few hours."

The guy was at work by then, and my parents would be suspicious if I came home suddenly sick. The only person I knew who lived nearby was Hannah. I considered the fact that we hadn't gotten into any especially bad screaming matches recently, so I took a chance and called her.

An hour later, I walked into Hannah's open doorway, where she had Gatorade and a blanket ready for me on her couch. She fed me and puttered off to do her laundry. We watched episodes of *Laguna Beach* in near silence until I felt okay enough to drive home. On the way to my car that afternoon, I passed her boyfriend—the one we all adored. He was getting home from work. I hugged him.

Even when I want to grab Hannah by the hair—then, by the pool, or now—I remember. Her feet in fuzzy pink socks, making me soup. The way her freckles multiplied after a day smoking joints on the beach. Her name, scrawled in Sharpie on a bathroom wall. This web of moments stretching and crisscrossing between us. I block out the men in my memories, but their presence is pressing in on the margins, always around.

You know it's not true, right? What I said before, that it's *no big deal.* But also, it is true. It has to be.

If we made a big deal of it now, if we started to list every instance of sexual violence that happened to us—individually, collectively, recently, or from the time we were girls—we would still be there, talking. We would start screaming and never stop.

~

In her book *I Hate Men,* Pauline Harmange constructs an argument in favor of misandry: the active dislike of men. She mentions that one risk (according to men, importantly) of misandry is that of alienating "good" men from the feminist movement.

"The accusation of misandry . . . It's to allege that a woman who hates men is as dangerous as a man who hates women—and that there's no rational justification for what she feels, be it dislike, distrust, or disdain. Because, obviously, no man has ever hurt a woman in the whole course of human history. Or rather, no men have ever hurt any women."

I read *I Hate Men,* a small book, in one sitting at a diner. A group of men at a table near mine were harassing their waitress. She responded to their beckons (She had to). She indulged their gross jokes, their holding ransom of her tip until she acquiesced and broke into a smile (She had to). One asked for her number, and after a pause and an awkward giggle, I heard her recite the digits (She had to).

Once they got up and left, I let the cover of my book fall open, its title in big, yellow letters splayed across the table. I realized I had been unconsciously covering it up with my hand (I had to).

The problem with the fact that I, too, hate men is that I love a man. I mean this literally, in that I am in love with a single human man: my husband. I also mean that I love A Man™, in the figurative sense, nebulously, most of the time. Cowboys, Paul Newman, a firm grip on soft flesh. I love the "good" ones, whatever that means (you know what it means). This complicates things for me, and for Harmange. She mentions her husband in a footnote: "Even though I love my husband and have never thought for a second of leaving him, I continue to reflect and insist upon my dislike of men. And to tar him with the same brush. I can do that, because life isn't simple."

I have heard every woman I know echo this sentiment—"I hate men"—verbally, symbolically, in varying degrees of outrage and sadness and confusion and annoyance. I think it's all true at the same time: I hate men, and I love men, and I love women and believe them when almost every single one of them says that a man has violated their autonomy in some way. I want both things to be true. But of course, they aren't. Mathematically, someone is lying; more good men must have done bad things than they are willing, or ready, to admit.

This idea gnaws at me. I wonder about the men in my life—my friends, my brothers, my dad, my uncles and grandpas and teachers and coaches. My own husband. What his answer might be if I asked him the question I want to ask of every man I meet: "Have you? Would you know it if you had?" He was also, once, a teenage boy, and this presents obvious problems. If I think about it for too long, it nauseates me. Would they tell me the truth? Would I believe them if they didn't?

But I can't get into all that now. I've just started making you believe me.

~

Of course not, I always thought, until then (until now, really).

Of course, rape *is not what happened to you.*

You had sex when you were too drunk all the time, I tell little Rachel.

But I was asleep, she says.

You made out with him before then, though. At that house show, in Bradenton, remember?

I was drunk then, too, stupid.

~

I told Emma about this, that day at the beach. That I'm trying to grapple with how often I form accusations against myself when I would never make them for other people. Every story of sexual assault that I read, I believe. I don't wonder if the writer had been complicit in any way. If she was exaggerating or misremembering or inferring or recovering false memories. I have never wondered, not once, if the writer was lying.

So why do I lie to me?

If anyone else was asking me these questions about something that had happened to them, it would drive me crazy; it would break my heart.

It is breaking my heart, in real time, how frustrating I am, how incapable of extending empathy, of giving her any grace. How I lack the discipline to write this correctly. I am still not telling it right.

I always resist the trauma plot, chafe against the idea that all women have sexual trauma, and so all women writers of nonfiction must write about their trauma, meaning all women's writing is about rape. If what Devo said is true, it changes things.

That's not even right, though, is it? If what Devo says I said is true—*he raped you*—then I have to change things. I have to change what I say about me. Now, I have to call myself "rape victim." A person who has been raped. *Ah-ha,* I get to say for now, if I choose not to believe what she says. *Not me.*

Of course, me. Of course, you. So what do we do now?

~

We call things "feral" when they contain some element of danger to us, when they show their teeth, when we want them to be something other than what they actually are. What's the difference between a feral cat and a wildcat? Between a thing that is wild and a thing that is simply free?

Perception. Language. Choice.

I've joked that when I do eventually die, I want a Viking funeral—my body lit on fire and pushed out to sea. A watery grave would suit me, I think. But I'm not dead yet. I'm still here, collecting wrinkles and gathering courage.

Here I am, all of this effort, a book with my name on it. I could be writing about anything, and right away, it's about *him*. Stupid, boring, nothing, little him. I'm annoyed that I am devoting so much page space to this one part of me. I'm angry that I'm supposed to be angry, that I'm supposed to be sad, that by writing this I am just one more log on the funeral pyre of serious engagement with our art, fulfilling the stereotype. I want to write nothing about it, to forget it, but everything makes me think about it all the time, even if I don't recognize it for what it is.

I hate that I know what she means, that now-famous other woman who probably wishes she could forget stupid, boring, nothing, little, red-faced him, when she says at a hearing in the highest court in the nation that it is "indelible in the hippocampus." It's clinging to me, to my gray matter, invading my personal and intellectual space. It bubbles up when I should be thinking about more important things, like writing, like having dinner with friends. It comes to me at random, his face—when I'm at Willow Tree Nursery buying a new fiddleleaf fig; when I'm sweating on a spin bike in a dark room while an EDM remix of a Britney Spears song blasts; when I'm driving past my high school football field where, you guessed it, another stupid, boring, little him did the obvious Bad Thing, and now I have to pull over, get out of the car, crouch in the grass with the fire ants, and name one thing I can see, one thing I can touch, and one thing I can hear until my breathing goes back to normal.

It ink-stains everything, erases all of my hard work. I don't want it to be the only story I can tell.

I want to be Suzie and Jennifer. I want to buy sailboats for them, and for all of my girlfriends—real and imaginary. I dream of a ragtag armada, a flotilla of undead girls who tell the truth. I want to be the girl from the trailer park who sails off into the sunset with all of the money, but with no wig, my grays starting to show, clad in a hot-pink bikini. A hot monument. Another force resistant to every man who saw something wild in a young woman and felt the urge to break it.

"Wild," of course, doesn't just mean untamed, out of control. It describes the natural order of things, when the influence of man is nowhere to be found—wilderness, wildlife, wildflowers. The miraculous persistence of things with sharp teeth and matted fur. Things that would not, could not, be beaten back, hemmed in, or brought into submission. They might be fucked up, missing an eye, sporting bald patches, scary. But their softness survived. A teenage girl is a monster, but in the same way, a teenage girl is a miracle.

Even now, I am trying to use all of these other things to tell my story for me because, very often, I do not feel like my own story is enough. I am trying to tell you, but I am also trying to convince myself, writing my own harpoon gun into existence. By telling you, I'm telling little Rachel too that maybe this is why we are the way we are, but it is not *who* we are. This is not the only story we can tell. But we have to tell them. To let it be wild, push it out to sea, so all of our other stories can come next.

spring break forever

Midway through *Spring Breakers,* the 2013 Day-Glo fever dream of a movie directed by Harmony Korine, three teenage girls in bright-pink bikinis and balaclavas are robbing a chicken shack. One of them is scared. One of the other girls says to her, "Just pretend it's a video game. Like you're in a fucking movie." Something shifts—a flicker behind the eyes under the mask. Then, the music picks back up, and the girls start screaming and brandishing their guns at the restaurant's patrons.

This scene, in a movie set and filmed in my hometown of St. Petersburg, Florida, was on my mind recently, on the day that the trailer for the newest *Grand Theft Auto* (GTA) video game hit the internet. The GTA trailer's scant ninety seconds contained references to what seemed like every single Florida meme in existence: airboats flying through the swamp, Miami high-rises glinting in the sun, computer-generated strippers shaking their pixelated asses while dollar bills flurried around them. A gigantic alligator waltzed into a convenience store, filtered through CCTV. It seems as if a visual shorthand has developed for cueing an audience that a story is taking place in Florida, which is certainly useful for a medium like a trailer: quick shots, the setting of a specific vibe that's meant to garner excitement for a longer-form project still to come. The game won't be out until long after I write this, so I have no idea if it will live up to fan expectations or defy my own.

Still, it makes perfect sense to me that Florida was chosen as the setting for a video game known for its gleeful indulgence in vice and violence. That's not to say I think that Florida is that sort of place in reality—mostly, it isn't—but if my lifetime as a Floridian has taught me anything, it's that most people don't actually care about reality when it comes to their vision of the state.

And really, why should they? For over a hundred years, Florida has been pitched as a paradise, a utopia, a place thoroughly unreal. Starting with the missives sent back to Spain by conquistadors; continued by the enterprising Henry Flagler, who laid train tracks and constructed palaces for the East Coast's gallivanting new-money crowds; and doubled down upon by the developers who promised escape to the mid-century families to whom they sold acres of swampland dressed up as an oasis.

I thought about the girls in the chicken shack, aiming their guns at the patrons. The strippers and convenience store owners and women selling *paletas* on Miami sidewalks. In the game and the movie, they're all NPCs, non-player characters. They spout off rote dialogue in cut scenes, repeat programmed movements on a loop. They are played by nameless extras in *Spring Breakers*. They are all Floridians.

If the reality you live in every day is projected back at you, on pages and screens and newspaper headlines, as an absurd un-reality, where does that leave you? Are you an NPC, or are you real?

~

When news broke that *Spring Breakers* was going to be filming in St. Pete, and that the crew was looking for extras, I remember the excitement that buzzed through town. In my early twenties, I worked at a beach bar known for its "College Night" and dollar shooters, and several of my fellow bartenders were frantic to swap shifts so they could go to the open call. A few of my friends from high school joined the throng, and when the movie came out a few years later, I was thrilled to see their faces on screen, if just for a fleeting second.

The director, Harmony Korine, is known for his ability to blend real people with professional actors, to blur the line between who is performing and who isn't. The slo-mo of the shot in question enhances the frenzied motion of a crowd of pretend vacationers, ironically played by a tourist town's permanent residents. The scene is excessive, soundtracked by a thumping Skrillex beat: red Solo cups are held aloft; bare breasts bounce in every direction, Mardi Gras beads ricochet off so much sunburnt flesh. Most of their eyes are hidden by neon sunglasses, and they flash wide smiles and stuck-out tongues. It's *The Garden of Earthly Delights* meets Girls Gone Wild. I didn't immediately recognize any of my friends' boobs, but that doesn't mean they weren't there. I asked my friend Kelly, many years later, if she remembered the day of the shoot (she has a brief appearance licking a popsicle behind a sand dune).

"You know, they wanted us to deep-throat one of those rocket pops, and I wouldn't do it," she said. She couldn't quite remember, she said, but she was pretty sure that the topless townie extras flashed the cameras of their own volition.

~

Harmony Korine's films have always been provocative, regardless of which side of the camera he has been on. *Kids,* a screenplay written by Korine when he was just eighteen and eventually brought to life by director, photographer, and producer Larry Clark, is critically acclaimed as much for its breakout performances by future A-listers

37

Chloë Sevigny and Rosario Dawson as it is for the grimy, morally vacuous state of most of its characters' psyches.

In the movie, a group of teenage boys skate, drink, and party their way around New York City unsupervised, wandering in and out of apartments, parks, and bodegas. They talk about sex constantly and treat the girls around them with indifference at best and active malevolence at worst. There are so many instances of dubious consent, assault, drugging, and rape that the viewer loses count. It's not an easy movie to stomach.

Larry Clark has said that when bringing Korine's screenplay to life, he wanted to make the Great American Teenage Movie. When I saw *Kids* years after it came out, as a teenager myself, I probably would have said he had done just that. For most of the movie, I thought it was a documentary—until I recognized Dawson, who I'd seen in *Men in Black II*. I'd never seen anything that got under my skin the same way *Kids* did. My opinion on Clark has shifted, but that movie still affects me on repeat viewing. I remember being glued to the screen on that first watch, alternately horrified and hit with shockwaves of recognition that left me melancholic. It struck me as one of the most truthful depictions of boy-girl relations I'd ever seen: a very different, dirty window into the story of teenagehood. It was honest about the inevitable loss of youthful innocence that so many other filmmakers sugarcoated or romanticized. (I don't know what that says about the kinds of boys, or girls, I hung out with.) It felt gross and clarifying, embarrassing for some reason—like someone was running a blacklight over my dirty sheets.

Of course, the parallels between me and my friends and the kids in *Kids* was not a one-to-one comparison. Korine likes to play in extremes of taboo, for entertainment and sometimes for shock value, that far exceed my own experiences. But after watching several of Korine's movies over the years, I got a sense that he understood what it was like to be from a misunderstood place. His characters are often motivated by desperation rather than ambition or any kind of hope for their futures. They're defiant and reckless and impulsive. Watching them feels like running your tongue over a cavity you forgot you had.

Many of the films he went on to make featured first-time amateurs scouted off the street, performing alongside more experienced actors. Korine's fondness for improvised dialogue and loose structure are unsettling in the best way, employing the elements of cinema verité to an extreme that leaves me disoriented. I don't always like his movies, but they always leave me thinking, re-evaluating what I thought I knew.

I think it's fair to call Korine "problematic." *Gummo,* in particular, is a movie I've never been able to rewatch. It's an onslaught of indefensible actions perpetrated by mostly irredeemable characters, and the visuals are so grimy as to almost have a smell and texture to them that leap off the screen. But that underlying rawness, a commitment to the bit that Korine is known for, pulls me past the surface and keeps me from writing him off. When filming *Gummo,* Korine used real locations in some of Nashville's poorest neighborhoods, including a home infested with roaches. Korine found it insulting to the local cast and homeowners when members of the crew requested that he supply them with hazmat suits, and he decided to direct in a Speedo and flip-flops "just to piss them off." His movies always feel like they are telling the truth, even if they make me nauseous.

The problem with *Spring Breakers* is that it bothers me on a more personal level, one that is harder to articulate. Not just the film itself—which has a mediocre cast and blown-out, saturated visuals that don't always work—but the actual circumstances of its existence. It bothers me that Korine set it in St. Pete. I feel protective of my city. Tourists *do* come here in droves every spring, so it makes sense, theoretically, to set the film here; but the visitors make for easy marks. Mostly, locals regard them with a blend of annoyance and begrudging gratefulness for their discretionary income, which drives our local economy. They're a buzz in the background, a swarm of lovebugs to be swatted away habitually during the months of November through May, when temperatures peak and the beaches become our own once again.

Growing up, I liked the beach the most then, once the spring breakers had left. Finally, we were free of the shell-searchers and moms casting dirty looks at the ratty sheet where my friends and I laid, blasting Trina's *Still da Baddest* album as we draped damp towels over our sandy heads to light our joints and Parliament Lights. At night, we'd ride up and down the beach, stopping at bars with names like Undertow and The Drunken Clam, chauffeured by the Free Beach Ride—a fleet of golf carts available by phone, driven by the same boys who worked the parasail stands and charter boats during the tourist season.

I never actually went on spring break, so to speak. I lived in Florida already and worked at the kinds of bars the girls in the movies went to. Where was I going to go, Myrtle Beach? No thanks. Our beaches were prettier, and I knew where to find secret parking spots at all of them. I was also a college dropout, and spring break as a concept only really works if, for the other weeks of the year, you are diligently attentive to your studies or in pursuit of some serious life goal. Sure, I wanted to be a writer, as a kind of daydream, but I had to pay my bills. Instead, I worked every kind of job: at bars; at a party store; as a voicemail transcriptionist in a strip-mall warehouse; and at a Bob Evans, where I had to fight octogenarian waitresses for tables during the after-church rush. I spent most of my time catering to the whims of people who had come here from other states for a *rumspringa* of the mind, body, and soul. My friends and I didn't get to be spring breakers, titular characters. We waited on them. We were just extras, licking popsicles.

~

Six years later, Korine released another movie set in Florida, *The Beach Bum*. When I saw that this next project starred Matthew Mc-Conaughey, Zac Efron, and Snoop Dogg, I was trepidatious. I'd felt so disillusioned by the *Spring Breakers* vision of Florida, the unreality of its premise, that I didn't want to get burned again. Nevertheless, I went to see *The Beach Bum* on opening weekend in 2019, many years after leaving Florida myself, at a packed theater in Brooklyn that served specialty cocktails and fifteen-dollar tater tots. I was homesick, and I hoped that seeing *The Beach Bum* in New York might give me some much-needed perspective: the ability to see Florida like an outsider.

In the movie, McConaughey plays Moondog, the titular beach bum who is now washed up and wrung out, having once made a name for himself writing poetry that everyone around him seems to think is gospel. Moondog is instantly lovable, a giggling stoner in a marabou-feathered dressing gown who gets away with a host of reprehensible actions. He is cheating on his rich wife Minnie (who is cheating right back with Snoop Dogg's character), stealing golf carts, escaping rehab, pushing an elderly woman in a wheelchair into a wall, ruining his daughter's wedding day, and pushing a tuba player off a dock into the water in Key West. Everything Moondog does is an intrusive thought. He has no real character arc: he does not grow or change or experience self-reflection in any real way. His actions cause chaos, anger, and even death in the lives of everyone around him, but they don't seem to have any real permanent effect on his sense of self or material reality. The main focus of his life, as he tells an interviewer toward the end of the movie, is to have fun.

"I am quite certain that the world is conspirin' to make me happy," he says. "Fun is the fuckin' gun, man." Moondog is the whooping GTA player at the console, careening through a candy-colored Florida set and mowing down NPCs while streetlights blur above him.

In a lot of ways, I think Harmony Korine is telling on himself in *The*

Beach Bum. Originally from Nashville, Korine has lived in Florida for the last decade or two, after making *Spring Breakers* and a few other small projects. I think it's his sly, sideways testament to the love he has developed for Florida. Instead of the harsh, fluorescent shock value that shapes the moral compass of *Spring Breakers, The Beach Bum* is all sunlight, golden hour, and the buzzy, warm neon signs in a dive bar.

Every time someone asks Moondog about his poetry, he recites a few lines that stun the listener, only to then divulge that it was actually D. H. Lawrence or Baudelaire prose he was passing along as his own. Throughout the hijinks of the movie, we see Moondog pecking away at his typewriter in montage, always writing, although the only original poetry we hear him read is unchanged from the first draft to a reading at the Pulitzer Prize ceremony (!) he attends in a women's evening gown after finishing his book (which multiple characters refer to as a novel, though he wins the prize for poetry. I'm not sure if Korine is making a layered joke about writing and prestige, or if he is doing that Korine thing where he may have just been too bored to Google it).

McConaughey is perfect in *The Beach Bum* because he already has a public reputation for fun-loving puckishness; it's not a stretch to see early footage of Moondog as a more buttoned-up, serious writer and visualize his descent into wild nihilism as parallel to McConaughey and Korine's own mutual love for straddling the line between art and entertainment. I can imagine that the real-life Harmony and Matthew might have had some interesting conversations about life, art, and writing.

McConaughey's memoir *Greenlights* sold like hotcakes, but I never read it for the same reason I don't like to watch interviews with Harmony Korine. When pushed to articulate their aesthetics, the men behind the art don't say any of the things I want to hear. McConaughey gets away with surface-level answers, I think, mostly because of his gaggle of Oscars and affable, "alright, alright, alright" persona. Korine takes an enfant terrible approach to most public appearances that bores the hell out of me. Depending on his mood, he's withdrawn and haughty, like the worst snob in your Film Studies 101 class, or he takes on a sort of manic skate-rat energy, answering questions with rambling digressions or straight-up dick jokes. He shows up on red carpets in robot masks and sailor hats and sometimes visibly coked out. Maybe this is life imitating art; maybe it's all a disguise for someone deeply afraid to be vulnerable except in their work, where his characters' big personalities and dumb antics cover up the wounds of addiction, religious trauma, poverty, and violence.

So, annoyingly, I love Harmony Korine, even though I find him deeply problematic. In some ways, his films taught me how to love, or how to think about love. Romantic love a little bit, sure, like how not to end up in love with a boy like Casper in *Kids*. But more than that, the thing I related to was Korine's devotion to his own vision, the relationship between the artist and their choice of subject. The cinematographer's love, the gaze that encompasses something others find ordinary and makes it special. Korine's gaze filters over Florida with the warm neon buzz of a 7–Eleven sign and clouds of weed smoke.

Automatic weapons were not *not* part of my life, but they weren't wielded by characters like *Spring Breaker*'s Alien. Played by James Franco, the role of Alien is clearly an homage to the rapper Riff Raff, with cornrow braids, a gold grill, and stockpiles of assault rifles. In my life, guns lived behind glass cabinets in houses owned by ultra-rich kids, in whose houses parties occurred. Franco's performance didn't bother me because it wasn't realistic; it was because it was *him* who was doing it: Franco, who went to NYU film school as a bit, or as a way to pick up the young coeds he is allegedly so fond of. You don't get to do that impression, I think; the same kind of heat rises in my cheeks when someone fakes a hillbilly accent. I feel a stubborn ownership of this kind of caricature, this fake-ass Florida Man that makes me feel so queasy.

I don't feel that way watching the scenes where Selena Gomez is sitting in a metal folding chair in a church circle, singing hymns; that feels familiar and I know that girl, dragged to church by a friend, unsure of the theology but deeply interested in the idea of congregation. I also literally know that girl: I forgot that my friend Marisa plays one of the youth group attendees, sitting in a chair a few down from Gomez's character Faith. It fucks with my head a little that the extras are real people, and the "real people" are Disney Channel stars. Korine's films contain both fantasy montages and realistic portraits of the way things are, and I think that's why I love them and hate them and want to live inside them. Moondog is the last of the barman poets; he's also a total fucking asshole. I've met a hundred Moondogs in Florida.

~

To me, *The Beach Bum* is almost a perfect movie, and watching it with some distance from *Spring Breakers* made me see the latter film much differently. It feels now like maybe Korine was practicing with *Spring Breakers,* warming up for something. Like how you climb the Empire State Building and see something bad and flashy on your first visit to New York City, but by the third or fourth year you actually live there, the place reveals itself to you in an almost holy way, like you've earned its trust. If *The Beach Bum* is a native Floridian diving on Big Pine Key, *Spring Breakers* is sunburnt and slurring outside Sloppy Joe's.

There are ten minutes of Franco hissing "Sprang break . . . sprang break for evaaaa . . ." through his grills, set over a montage of his character Alien playing the Britney Spears song "Sometimes" on a giant piano at sunset on the Intracoastal. It's all a little much. In contrast, thirty seconds of Moondog silently cuddling a wharf cat can almost bring me to tears in its simple, lovely framing. The pink ski-masked nymphettes of *Spring Breakers* ring false, not because they're in string bikinis and Dunks, but because they were created by a man who hadn't fully fallen in love yet. He was still a tourist himself. Tellingly, as the girls take a bus from school to their spring break destination, there is an anachronism that only someone from this part of Florida would catch: the bus they are on crosses the Skyway heading in the wrong direction, north instead of south.

In *The Beach Bum,* Moondog is headed absolutely nowhere. He is a washed-up, whacked-out, white man who commits too many crimes to list during the course of two cinematic hours. The *Spring Breakers* are criminals, wild girls in search of a better life by any means necessary, but Moondog gets to be a poet. He knows he has a better life than he deserves, but he doesn't let that stop him from pursuing ever-greener pastures, chasing "fun, the fuckin gun," regardless of who he estranges or maims along the way.

His poetry is not good; it's his charismatic performance of the poem that makes people love it. But it's a product of a lifetime of hedonism in a place that specializes in such a pursuit. When he performs it in a dive bar, people hoot and holler, fellow Floridians seeing the silliness in its prose. When he wins a prize and reads it in front of a room full of high-society literature critics, it's suddenly profound. It makes sense to me that this is the Florida Man Korine has created—a hedonist who lugs around a typewriter and occasionally strikes gold when he reaches an audience at the right time. Moondog gets away with everything, escapes any kind of consequence, always lands on his feet. In this way, Moondog is the truest Floridian man I can think of, at least in the cinematic imagination. He is an unreal person in an unreal place.

the last resort

There's a bar near Daytona, off the side of State Road A1A, called The Last Resort. It sits atop a patch of scraggly lawn, squat and brick and foreboding. From the limbs of an oak tree behind the building hang several busted and rusted motorcycles, suspended by heavy chains.

The bar advertises itself on Facebook as "The Home of Ice Cold Beer and Killer Women." This became their claim to fame when a regular at The Last Resort, a woman named Aileen, drank some of those ice-cold beers—Miller Lites, actually. She played Randy Travis on the jukebox and shot some pool with the other patrons, most of whom knew her well. The owner of the bar later told the *Miami New Times* that this woman "kept to herself . . . she was quiet and never messed with anyone." That night would be Aileen's last as a free woman.

Before that, though, she joined in one of the bar's oldest traditions: with a cigarette still dangling from her mouth, she removed her bra and hung it, with dozens of others, over the crumbling wooden beams above the pool tables of The Last Resort. Littered among them were the typical Florida-dive-bar ephemera: scrawled-on dollar bills, Gasparilla beads, bumper stickers, and local motorcycle club patches. Two men came up to her, pretended to solicit her for sex work and offered to buy her a motel room. These men, who were in fact undercover cops, walked one of America's first female serial killers, the "ice-cold" Aileen Wuornos, out of the bar and straight into federal custody.

I've driven A1A dozens of times. The long state highway begins in Key West and winds all the way up to Amelia Island, the Atlantic Ocean's endless blue flickering in and out of view through the passenger-side window. It's dotted with endless condos, beach houses, bait shops, tourist traps, and shitty little bars like The Last Resort every few miles. A1A passes through Miami Beach with its throngs of off-duty influencers, then winds along the brain-dead suburbs of Hollywood and the gilded, evil streets of Palm Beach. These streets turn into avenues, branching into wide driveways where the New York expats of Boca Raton park their luxury hatchbacks. Motorists along A1A, with their eyes to the skies, can spot the Kennedy Space Center beyond the broken-down fruit stands strewn across the highway as they continue north, above which billionaires launch themselves into the future. It continues along the weed-scented shores of Cocoa Beach, the last bastion of the puka shell necklace. I like to take a long last look at the young bodies arcing their surfboards over the glittering seafoam before the highway carries me deep into the past.

A1A emerges, then, onto the cobblestones of America's oldest city. I scan for the Bridge of Lions, built by the Spanish when they first settled the town known as St. Augustine and erected their seashelled fortress, whose coquina walls absorbed cannonballs as softly as if they were navel oranges. Patinated plaques grace the side of the roadway every few feet, it seems, indicating this or that centuries-old monument or another historic site: the settling and renaming of other peoples' land. Not far from Ripley's Believe It or Not! on San Marco Avenue stands the alleged site of Juan Ponce de Leon's Fountain of Youth. The average traveler could be forgiven for not seeing the sad, trickling stream there—reeking of sulfur—as a miracle.

The palm trees start to descend in number as I drive even further north, and the live oaks take over, their Spanish moss hanging down like little branch-beards, moving back and forth in the lazy wind. The road starts to incline. The billboards for crisis pregnancy centers increase in number. More pecans decorate the exit signs than cartoon alligators as the roadway begins ramping up to meet I-95, then I-10, and the hills of South Georgia.

Along this highway, down backroads and turnoffs and rest stops, in the middle of the night and very early in the morning, Aileen Wuornos murdered at least seven men who stopped to solicit her for sex work. She claimed that the murders had been in self-defense, after these men pushed her beyond her limits or violently assaulted her. At her trial, she said, "Well, if you can't be a good example, be a horrible warning." A year and a week after her arrest at The Last Resort, Aileen was sentenced to death by lethal injection.

~

It might surprise you to know that Aileen and I have a few things in common. I think about those things more than I should.

Like Aileen, I, too, love Randy Travis. I danced with my husband to one of his songs at our wedding, promising to love him "forever and ever, amen" as Category-5 Hurricane Irma churned toward us, just miles away. Our wedding guests were jovial but edgy, a manic energy falling over the dozens of attendees who had either been brave enough to stay put or were headed north on evacuation routes anyway.

My vows were scribbled on the back of a grocery list, the most un-self-conscious writing I may have ever done. I was too preoccupied to let them get long. His were the most beautiful words I've ever heard. My brothers filled in as the missing best men, and in doing so became mine forever. My sister, carrying my growing niece in her belly, eight months along, stood behind me, as she always has, radiant and apple-cheeked in the September heat. The sun shone the whole time we vowed. Not a cloud in the sky. We ate boiled peanuts and chicken biscuits, and my cousin from Arkansas got proposed to while I was distracted.

Later, Adam told me that an enormous bee had circled my head and my bouquet for the entire ceremony. I never saw it, too starry-eyed by my conviction and his Star Search smile to care about anything else. For his part, he had pretended not to notice, knowing how frayed my nerves were that day as call after call from guests and vendors and family members came in—their flights canceled, highways in standstill traffic, their elderly parents and babies needing to be cared for and worried about. He looked at a circling threat, however small and irritating, and grinned it out of existence.

We shut it down early, sensing the wind and humidity changes in our bones like only people who have lived through tropical storms can. Everyone loaded into their cars in high heels and suits, wedding favors taking their place next to flashlights loaded with fresh batteries, gallons of distilled water, and board games. My new husband and I drove through the night in a rental car, alternately flying across the highway and crawling along traffic-jammed state roads, nervously eyeing the gas gauge and the clock, barely talking, as the storm chased us. I only breathed a sigh of relief when, ascending, we saw the state recede out of the tiny window. We disappeared into the clouds, toward our future, finally free of the storm. Randy Travis's words about forgetting things you know rang through my head. As much as I missed Florida, I was grateful to be escaping such a familiar panic, all the hurricanes I had weathered before. What a gift to be able to finally fly away, back to New York, to my new life.

So, both country music fans and both married, Aileen and I—that's another thing we share, although her nuptials were short-lived. Her husband was in his seventies, she hit him with his cane, and he filed a restraining order against her. Apples and oranges, really.

Both fake blondes who used to be real ones when we were little girls, whenever that was. We were both the result of unwanted pregnancies, but this is another common place where our paths twist away from one another. We were both breech births, adding injury to the original insult of our presence in the wombs of our mothers. Tiny feet yet to step onto the cold ground of this indifferent state, pointing out first instead of our heads. "She was born ass-backwards," my uncle used to say about me, "and she's been that way ever since."

We both eventually made it out of Florida, albeit in different ways—me in a rented car, escaping to New York City in my early twenties; her in a body bag at just forty-six.

In his foreword to *Monster: My True Story,* an unauthorized biography of Aileen, the author Christopher Berry-Dee talks only briefly of the monstrosity of Aileen's life before the murders. He says that his ultimate goal in writing the book was not sensationalism, but to shed light on the flaws of the criminal justice system, to show the hard work and diligence of the cops involved in Aileen's case.

I don't buy it. The book is co-credited to her, but Aileen hated cops, had since she was little, when they failed to do anything to stop the obvious abuse she suffered at the hands of almost every single man she came into contact with, or had the bad luck of being blood-related to. Berry-Dee does say something toward the end of the foreword that I snag on, though, that strikes me as profound in a way the author almost certainly did not intend. But I think about his words every time I compare the way my life played out against Aileen's path: "When one sets out to investigate the road to murder, well signposted as it may be, one finds diversions, small, seemingly insignificant dirt roads that can lead to unexpected discoveries. Aileen Carol Wuornos led her eight victims into such diversions where they expected something less than being blasted to death. This book will take you down those roads to a place where you will never look back."

~

One thing most people can't say: I got my first period in the Everglades.

I was on a school trip, part of an educational program called "Nature's Classroom" that took public school students to state parks and preserves. The idea, I think, was that children could learn about Florida's flora and fauna up close and personal and foster some sense of civic pride. It was the nineties, and we were still optimistic about conservation. The trip bought our parents a weekend of peace anyway, and that is how, in the name of ecology, my eighth-grade class boarded a charter bus headed southeast-bound over the Skyway Bridge, down into the heart of the swamp. I crept, oblivious, one exit sign at a time, closer to my womanhood. A kind of Sword of Damocles bumped gently, invisibly, above my head as we moved south down the map.

The important part of this story isn't me getting my period, though, not really. I tell that part in my mind all the time. I get that it icks people out or prevents certain men from continuing to read this story. I don't need to tell it for it to be important to me. But I think about it at weird times, especially when I am alone or if I find myself staring up at a streetlamp, buzzing sunset-colored in the nighttime Florida heat that pays no mind to the changing of seasons. There's a story there, a hazing or a haunting, I'm not sure. Something about the moon and the tides, the swamp and the street, but people don't like to hear that story in barrooms and backyards.

We got to Everglades National Park and settled into our thatched-roof cabins. I felt a weird twinge, a stabbing feeling, while unpacking my pajamas. My flashlight and I took a little trip out of the cabin, toward the fluorescent-lit public bathroom, swatting away mosquitoes on the dimly lit path. I eased a rusted latch, stepped in, and eased it shut again.

Then—red. No cinematic moment. No revelations. No angels singing or symbolic lady-flower unfurling. Just a sweaty campground bathroom, panic, and a stomachache that bent me double. Eventually, I found an adult—my gifted teacher, Miss Burgess, a wavy-haired hippie who wore batik dresses and Tevas and grew her own loofah plants. The charter bus took a motley trio out of the park and into the night: her, me, and our school's charter bus driver, a stocky woman with a Nextel walkie-talkie phone and little regard for my womanly plight. The carpeted seats of the bus were depressingly empty. I didn't know where to sit. The two grownups sat at the front of the bus, talking in hushed tones. I meandered toward the back, head hung low, thighs chafing in my jean shorts as I walked bow-legged like a cowboy to avoid what I assumed was a deluge of blood cascading, unseen, from deep within me. I sat down gingerly toward the back, hoping I might disappear into the seat like Alex Mack.

I did not disappear.

As we crept past the ranger's hut at the front of the state park, I imagined what my friends were doing in our cabin, back at the park. My stomach still hurt. In my head, I couldn't help but count the secrets being divulged by the minutes while I was gone on this stupid, embarrassing ride. I wanted to be anywhere but here. The highway lights rose and fell over my reflection in the mirrored surface of the bus windows, like I was in my own personal music video.

Eventually, we turned off the highway and into a brightly lit gas station parking lot. Miss Burgess called my name, and I walked to the front of the bus as if to my grave.

"Do you want me to go in with you?"

The question amazed me. I was fourteen at a Flying J on the side of the highway in the deepest part of South Florida, with no clear idea of what I was going into the gas station's convenience store to obtain.

I looked past my teacher's face toward the parking lot from the top step of the bus. I wasn't afraid, exactly; I'd played enough "Hey, Mister" with my friends at the 7–Elevens and Albertsons stores around town to lose any initial fear of strangers, especially the convenience-store kind. I don't really remember the store itself, buying pads, who paid for them, or whatever happened inside. But I do remember walking down that little set of stairs, the pneumatic noise of the bus doors opening and then closing behind me, setting foot on asphalt, and looking up into the streetlamps. I wasn't in the swamp anymore, but in my heart, I was lost in the wilderness.

On that quiet, late ride back, I sat in the seat next to Miss Burgess. I could tell she was uncomfortable, but that she felt either an urge or an obligation to be maternal. I didn't want or need her to be motherly, though, and I didn't really know how my own mother would have behaved if she had been there. Still, it felt rude to sit far away from her after she'd been part of what I knew would probably be a formative experience. We rode in silence for a while until suddenly the bus driver cleared her throat, glancing at us in the rearview mirror.

"A lot of the swamp people around here believe a lot of stuff about the moon, and the land, and all that. Like the tides and mangroves, shit like that. Maybe it means something, you getting your . . ." Here, she mumbled and then coughed a wet, nicotine cough. "Your cycle, you know, while it's a full moon."

I looked down at my lap.

"Maybe," Miss Burgess said. She patted my leg, weakly. "Maybe it doesn't mean anything at all."

~

Aileen Wuornos was a Pisces, born on leap day, perpetually skipped over. When I think about a young Aileen, I imagine her transparent—a dotted line around the space on the calendar, a shadow where a silhouette should be. Obviously, I am leading you here, with these similarities. I do not aspire to be like Aileen Wuornos. When I start looking for them, they appear one after another, but the ways in which we are similar do not make us the same. I've never killed anyone—or hit them with a cane, for that matter. Charlize Theron has certainly never won an Academy Award for playing me in a movie—for gaining thirty brave pounds and wearing fake, fucked-up teeth. Though she would've had to do both of those things were she cast in the story of my life. Charlize is tall and thin, and another thing Aileen and I have in common is a fondness for Miller Lite.

It scares me a little bit to think about us as connected. It thrills me a little too. We are also both rape survivors. I think she'd agree with me that the word "survivor" is doing a lot of heavy lifting. I think she'd also agree with me that "victim" doesn't tell the whole story either. The term does nothing for us, gives us no quarter, no special treatment in court or in a church pew or in a classroom. It provides no solace, no answers. It's just a noun.

Aileen's mother was fourteen at the time she was born, and the pregnancy was the result of a sexual assault by her family's adult handyman. Aileen's biological father was arrested not long after her birth for the kidnapping and rape of another minor, a seven-year-old girl. He hung himself in prison. When Aileen was around four years old, her mother asked Aileen's grandmother to watch her two children and never came back. Aileen and her brother were raised by their grandparents, and by all accounts, all parties involved were not willing participants.

I wonder if it matters to anyone but me that young Aileen was made to clean and condition the leather of the belt that her grandfather beat her with, often and viciously. That he told her she wasn't worth the air she breathed while he did so. Do you feel any differently about her crimes when you know that she was drinking by the age of twelve, that she started having sex with boys from her neighborhood in exchange for food? These same boys once threw her out of a moving van, badly injuring her head.

Very often, I envy Aileen. I wonder what it would feel like to kill the men who hurt me. Maybe that sounds extreme, but consider for a moment the fact that I have to use the plural there—men, not man. To be a woman who has been assaulted is to learn how to live with constant, indescribable, near-overwhelming rage. Rage that animates you, propels your limbs out of bed when you'd rather sink into the earth's core. Rage that threatens to ruin your life all over again when it surfaces at the slightest prompting. Rage that makes you watch trial footage of an unrepentant woman, accused of murdering seven men. A woman who showed up at her grandfather's funeral, the funeral of a man who was also the father of her own miscarried child, just to blow cigarette smoke in the corpse's face. My rage makes me exhale right along with her. This kind of rage will make you read these facts and think, *I get it.* Had things been only slightly different for me, I might have found myself on the wrong side of A1A some dark night, nothing to my name but sheer force of will and desperation. I feel pretty confident that the chances of my mugshot making the nightly news were always slim, but they were never zero.

~

On a rainy day in college, when I was about twenty, I decided to watch the movie *Monster*. At the time, I lived in Gainesville, Florida, home to two other famous killers. Ted Bundy, handsome devil, spent some time here, and a man named Danny Rolling, otherwise known as the Gainesville Ripper, murdered five students in the nineties. The movie offered me something to do that wasn't a football game or a frat party, in a town where there wasn't much else to do besides those things. It was a college town surrounded on all sides by rural Florida, farmland and biker bars just a few miles down Waldo Road. Sometimes drifters came through and stopped at the pool hall where I bartended when I wasn't in class, blowing menthol smoke in fat clouds across the bar while I opened their longnecks. The day in question was my day off, and I rode my bike from my apartment down to the punk-rock video store and rented the DVD of *Monster* from a scrawny guy in a Black Flag T-shirt. He looked at me suspiciously. I took it home and retreated to my room.

Seeing Charlize in poor-people drag felt strange and familiar at the same time. There was a scene in the movie where Aileen was at a gas station, attempting to freshen up between johns. Hers was a body I recognized instantly: soft at the belly, strong everywhere else. Long arms with tapered shoulders. Home-bleached hair, dark at the roots. She wore dirty bikini briefs, puckered at the elastic waistband. That harsh view, of that kind of body, made me want to put my hand in front of the screen. Aileen's body looked a little like mine. The leg holes of her Hanes sagged around the soft flesh that I share, what I've heard called "baby-bearing hips." I felt something hot and sludgy under my skin when I saw Charlize-as-Aileen giving herself an "airplane bath," something I've done several times at rest stops and campsites as a kid: soap pumped from the dispenser and rubbed under the armpits and down the front, "two wings and the tail." I could tell I was supposed to be nauseated by the scene, but it just made me sad.

Aileen, of course, was not the only Florida woman to commit horrible crimes. Something about her inspires a uniquely vitriolic feeling, though—my guess is that it has to do with her appearance, her poverty, her existence on the margins. She was not especially nice to look at, or listen to. One would think this doesn't matter, but time has shown us it does.

Years later, I watched another movie, one where a real-life woman was again portrayed by an Oscar-winning actress. In *May December,* Julianne Moore plays a fictionalized version of Mary Kay LeTourneau, a schoolteacher infamous for sleeping with and bearing the child of her underage student. The film follows the "couple" as adults, while another actress studies Moore's character for the upcoming biopic she will play her in. At times, it's hard to tell if the movie is a comedy or a drama. Moore is gorgeous, of course, and with the passage of time, the age gap is seemingly less severe. But the young man, who was a child when he met this woman, clearly feels the dissonance and struggles with the memory of who he was and what he could have been.

Florida has its own version of this story, of course. Debra Lafave was a middle school teacher in Temple Terrace when she groomed and raped a fourteen-year-old student. Lafave was blonde and blue-eyed and had dated a Backstreet Boy in high school. The media went crazy, with headlines like "Hot for Teacher," and pictures of her on a motorcycle in a bright-blue bikini made the rounds. Many years later, a man named Joe Zuniga met Debra through his sister, who worked with her at a community health center. He found Lafave, who he called "Debbie," intriguing. Eventually, she agreed to let him write about her; the ensuing biography is titled *A Crown of Beauty for Ashes.* Its cover is a soft-focus photo of a blonde, blue-eyed woman, gazing at a monarch butterfly perched on her forefinger. It has quite a different story to tell about its subject than *Monster* does about Aileen. The book's synopsis, from its Amazon listing:

"Debra Jean Beasley LaFave is known to the world as a beautiful monster, a seductive pervert, a lovely wrecker of lives. How difficult must it be to live in a world that views you in such extreme polarities? When the media portrays someone as a sex object, or worse as a monster; it is easy to forget that that person developed over time. The story of 'now' overshadows the story of 'then.' It is only when the dust has settled and the news outlets are looking for ways to boost their ratings that the backstory is investigated and considered."

I remember the media coverage of Lafave, how they spoke about her. One news outlet declared her "too pretty for prison." During the subsequent trial, her attorney argued that putting Lafave in jail would be "like throwing meat to the lions."

Absolutely no one ever said that about Aileen.

The information I can find about Aileen's early life calcifies something inside me. The volume of violence visited upon this one young woman is staggering. It's not hard to see why she went crazy—why so many of us do.

In the movie version of her life, right before Aileen is apprehended outside The Last Resort, she runs into Tom, the veteran landlord of the storage unit she was living in sporadically. Tom sees a "Wanted" sketch of what is clearly Aileen on the bar's TV, has known, probably for some time, what is going on, and tries in his way to level with her.

Tom: "That's where you landed, that's what you had to do. What you're feeling right now is just guilt over something that you had absolutely no control over. You know how many of us came back from the war and almost killed ourselves because we felt exactly the same thing you do right now?"

Aileen: "Yeah?"

Tom: "Yeah. And they'll never get it. They don't get it now, they'll never get it then, and they sure as hell won't ever get fucking circumstance."

Aileen: "Fuck, man, circumstance. That's exactly it. You know, it's like I feel like I never had a fucking choice."

I wonder about that circumstance a lot. It unsettles me, how much I care for Aileen. I know I am supposed to be disgusted by her, afraid of her frizzed-out hair and wild eyes and her declarations, at her trial, that she would do it again. But I just feel guilt and a strange, sad kinship.

Where did I take a right turn, one that led me down the path I am on, where so many others were forced left—often without a choice? Why did I get the loving mother and the husband who distracts me from buzzing threats instead of dark highways and armed robbery?

I was poring over police reports and details about the night Aileen was finally taken in when I came across a snippet of information that made me pause. The last song she played on the jukebox at The Last Resort was Randy Travis. This, I knew already, but it was the name of the song that caught me by the throat. It was "Diggin' Up Bones." Not one of Randy's major hits, to be sure. The title sent a little chill down my spine, connecting it with Aileen who was responsible for the animated, living bodies of seven people being reduced to bones. But the song isn't actually about murder; it's about memories and the pointlessness in trying to rehash the details of something you've long let go. Her wedding ring, a negligee, everything a woman left behind on the way toward something or someone else.

I wonder what I'm trying to prove, showing that I empathize with a woman who did monstrous, unforgivable things. I may not have been as monstrous as her, but I felt like it, often. I understand what it feels like to be out of options. To feel like no one understands your pain. I felt it too. The rapid deterioration of a sense of self, the gnawing hopelessness. The difference between our trajectories is, I guess, arbitrary. Luck of the draw, fate, some cosmic dice roll. Circumstance. Thankfully, I have words. Sometimes they help. Sometimes they make it way worse. What I think I want to say winds away from me, always just beyond my headlight beams. Sometimes I sit down and someone else appears—some other, younger me who wants to talk instead. I relate to Randy, who sings about digging up things that you should just leave alone. Writing about myself sometimes gets a little spooky, like drinking with a ghost. I don't like staying too long in that world, one where I should probably be dead but have gotten away with the opposite of murder, which is the incredible feat of keeping myself alive.

At times, especially when I am driving down dark highways like A1A and passing some roadside bar, I think about Aileen and Florida and The Last Resort. There's something about Florida highways in the middle of the night that I find soothing. Maybe it started with that weird bus ride through the Everglades. Once I got my driver's license and my own car, it became a ritual, almost. When I can't sleep, when I'm trying to work my head around an essay or existential crisis, I grab the keys, a fountain soda from the gas station, and find the nearest on-ramp. I do my best thinking with the windows down, my hands and feet occupied with the muscle memory of driving. I look out the window and twist the dial, navigate the static, searching for clarity of voice.

I wonder if I think about the past too much, if I'm romanticizing it or making it a tragedy. At the time, it was just my life. It wasn't a narrative, just a series of choices moment to moment. But this is the work of writing about yourself, I think—looking for patterns, the subtext underneath those choices, contextualizing who you were and who you might have been.

On this night, I am thinking again about the choices that separated me from Aileen—my circumstance, so to speak. I play back the tape in my head. As much as I may outwardly joke about my wild years, as much as I beat myself up in private about my own recklessness and naïveté, the truth is less easily explained. The main difference between Aileen and me isn't one I can claim credit for, really. But I always felt a sense of certainty that I, myself, was not ice-cold. By some dumb luck, I found that I could still be soft, open to the world. If I could find a well-lit place, maybe better things awaited me. If I could just make it through the night. In the darkest parts of my life, through the mangroves and the buzzing bar lights, my own voice was whispering to me from the future, maybe from this car gliding over the asphalt right now, saying, "No stopping. This is not our exit."

"it is a queer place"

St. Augustine, Florida, feels like a town unstuck in time. It's my favorite place in Florida, outside of my hometown. Decades before the first Englishman ever set foot on Plymouth Rock, people of all creeds and nationalities crossed paths along the Atlantic Coast to establish trade routes, form religious groups, and till the land and see what bounties it might provide. Now, in the twenty-first century, I can travel there by automobile from Tampa in about four hours, cruising along the interstate with boiled peanuts in my lap. I love taking the back roads there and watching the modernity of my side of Florida, the west coast, fade away into more historic architecture and the bright waters of the Atlantic. This pilgrimage of my own would probably shock those early Floridians and conquistadors, how easy it is to time travel.

Part of what makes St. Augustine so special to me are the remnants of its storied past that remain and have become the hallmarks of the town's charm. The Bridge of Lions leading into the historic downtown is decorated with the Medici lions, two leonine protectors named Firm and Faithful and built to resemble their original versions in Florence. The crumbling ruins of Fort Matanzas stand picturesque against the blue sky above the Matanzas River, captured by hundreds of iPhones a day. There's a Dunkin' Donuts and a vape shop a few yards away from the St. Augustine History Museum, where throngs of tourists wait their turn to enter a pirate-themed escape room, where the puzzles center around buried treasure and cannonballs. App-enabled parking meters line the street curving alongside the St. Francis Barracks, originally fashioned by monks from centuries-old, crushed coquina shells. The past is everywhere, cartoonified at the same time as it is romanticized.

It makes sense that the town itself would change many times over, shape-shift depending on which masses were moving through its streets throughout history. No man steps on the same cobblestone twice, as it were, and no two people walking the streets of America's oldest city could have experienced it the same way. Their perception of St. Augustine depended entirely on who they were and, more importantly, *when* they were.

I think about this whenever I visit, as was the case a few years ago, when I stumbled upon a historical mystery that changed the way I would walk those streets afterward. I was doing a project for a graduate course, and my research led me to a selection of journal entries written by Ralph Waldo Emerson, published by his children after his death. These parts of Emerson's journals were special because they documented the years he lived in St. Augustine, having been sent there in the hopes that the warm air would ease his consumption symptoms.

As part of the class, we were to take a "literary pilgrimage"—visit the place where the text lives, learn how to access archives, consider the place along with the prose, and situate it in its cultural and physical landscape. The true, original pages of Emerson's journals were housed at a Harvard library, but I wasn't about to go to Boston for any reason. Besides, that felt contrary to the project. I wanted to read Emerson's words where they were written. Luckily, the St. Augustine Historical Society had a very early copy and some other documents related to the writer's time in Florida. So, a few awkward phone calls with the society's lovely (but reclusive) historians later, an afternoon appointment was made and to St. Augustine I went.

The library was housed almost in secret behind a beautiful garden, up a flight of wooden stairs, and through a door with an ancient buzzer that leads down a hallway to what could be an insurance office, except for all of the books and important papers and a faint air of White Diamonds. A kind young man escorted me to a table, where he had prepared a stack of books and a manila folder with everything the library possessed related to the years Ralph Waldo Emerson had spent in St. Augustine. He asked if I needed anything else, then left me to my homework.

I spent the better part of a Friday at a long table in that library, poring over the journals and documents. The room was quiet, with only the occasional ring of the telephone in the office adjacent to the reading room and the sounds of trolley cars racketing down the narrow alley behind the building. A guide on the trolley's PA system could be heard from the creaky leather chair where I sat, his voice lilting through the open window, describing the architectural styles of the historic block and recounting old ghost stories. I read a description of the very place I was visiting, written almost two centuries ago, with increasing wonder.

Around lunchtime, surprisingly moved by the archives, I decided to take a break and start a bit of a personal quest. I wanted to find out more about this oldest colony of Florida, which always occupied my imagination as a kid. The alleged Fountain of Youth, Henry Flagler, the fort. They made the Florida I was from, further south—all strawberry farms and suburbs—seem like it mattered. Like it was part of *actual* history, not just the footnotes. I decided to check out the Lightner Museum, which occupies the former Hotel Alcazar building, built in 1888.

Walking there, I passed Flagler College, wishing I had possessed the foresight or money to enroll there after graduating high school. The campus looked like it had been transported whole-cloth from Seville, its rust-red buildings with arched windows and wrought-iron gates lining the block. I crossed the street and walked down the long court-yard in front of the museum, feeling that if I squinted my eyes slightly and ignored the sheen of sweat gathering at my hairline, I might actually be in Europe. As it happened, though, my phone buzzed in my pocket. It was an Instagram notification alerting me that I'd been tagged in a post decrying the passing of House Bill 1557—colloquially known as the "Don't Say Gay" bill. I went from squinting to closing my eyes, sighing deeply. *Nope. Definitely still in Florida.*

I've always believed I would make a very good rich person, but once inside the museum, my belief became conviction. The main floor houses an exhibition called "The Gilded Age: Treasure of the Lightner Museum" in what was once the hotel's grand ballroom. It's a collection of seemingly random objects, until you realize that the reason for their being displayed together is the prestige of their ownership, not any artistic throughline. Murano glass, Victorian ceramics, early Quaker furniture—it's just dead rich people's shit. Still, I walked around the galleries like a street urchin, trying to eat everything with my eyes.

The second area of the museum is up the stairs—a gallery that is, actually, an extended balcony—sort of like a giant wraparound porch with an open middle. Leaning on the rail, you can look down onto a giant space filled with café tables and chairs. The museum's restau-rant sits at the bottom of the now-drained pool, where oil barons and wealthy widows came to revive themselves during bitter New England winters.

One of the photographs in this area caught my eye: a film still showing the exterior of the museum, as well as the Hotel Ponce de Leon across the street, which is now the same college campus I'd just been pining over. I read the placard next to the photo and found a reference to an early silent movie titled *A Florida Enchantment*. I made a note to look up the movie later and continued my walk around the gallery, imagining myself in the black-and-white photos in another life. Maybe I'd be somewhere in the background in a smart "bathing costume" and kohl eyeliner, hobnobbing with an Astor nephew, having just taken a steam train in from some lush lawn on Long Island to vacation in a state just beginning to be a destination.

After making my way out of the exhibit, I bought some coasters and a postcard at the gift shop. At the checkout counter, there was a bin of stickers—kryptonite for my wallet. Among the selection of Hemingway quotes and cartoon alligators was one in the shape of Florida, patterned in the rainbow flag. A small pink heart sat on the top right side, over St. Augustine's location.

At my Airbnb that night, I decided to look up the movie I saw mentioned on the placard. On YouTube, I found an upload of the movie titled "A Florida Enchantment (1914) First Lesbian movie ever!"— which piqued my curiosity. When the title cards listed a character as a "colored maid," I started to worry, and my suspicions were quickly confirmed. The film employed actors in blackface to play the roles, in the very first shot. It freaked me out, and I wasn't that curious, so I turned the movie off and tried to get some sleep before spending another day digging through my new friend Ralph's dusty diary.

~

Emerson was sent to our warm shores at the advice of his doctors in 1827, while ill with consumption in his early twenties. At the time, young Ralph was a Unitarian minister, dreaming of a life serving God with his words. There's a reverence to his writing about the place he found himself, but there's disdain and humor too. His first few entries, made after a week in town, strike a descending, if observantly funny, tone. He compares the locals to barnacles:

> "Whosoever is in St. Augustine resembles what may be also seen in St. Augustine, the barnacles on a ledge of rock which the tide has deserted ; move they cannot ; very uncomfortable they surely are; but they can hear from afar the roaring of the waters, and imagine the joy of the barnacles that are bathed thereby."

I'm not sure if he means that they are sedentary by choice or that they are simply abandoned, but I can imagine the reasons for his projection. His diaries and letters home from that period paint a vivid picture of a St. Augustine where Minorcans, newly freed Black Americans, conquistadors, expats, slave traders, Native Floridians, and Spanish emissaries all inhabited the same city limits. He says the city, its contours, the food and smells, are like nothing else he'd experienced. In a letter to his brother William, he says:

> "The air and sea of this ancient, fortified, dilapidated sand-bank of a town are really delicious . . . It is a queer place. What is done here? Nothing . . . I stroll on the sea-beach and drive a green orange over the sand with a stick. Sometimes I sail in a boat, sometimes I sit in a chair. I read and write a little, moulding sermons for an hour which may never arrive."

Twenty-three, ill, far from home, I can sense his frustration, maybe powerlessness. I was struck by the image of a young Emerson doing things I'd done so many times as a Floridian teen—walking the beach, idling, reading and writing with a view of the ocean. I liked thinking of this great man, with the stern face I'd seen in textbooks, rolling an orange across the sand, bored as any other young person on a vacation they didn't want to take. I tried to decide what kind of bathing suit he might wear today (my best guess: sensible board shorts, New-England navy). He notes in his letters home that his health is improving, slowly, that he's gained twelve ounces, up to a hefty 152 pounds. I imagine what he ate to get there, if they are the same things I like to eat when I visit: fried fish sandwiches, Minorcan stew with peppers and mussels. I wonder what he would think about the retro-hipster decor of The Ice Plant, a local craft cocktail bar lit by Edison bulbs, its cheeky old-timey toilet with a chain-pull flusher in the ladies' room.

Just before the Florida portion of Emerson's journals end, an interesting thing happens to the timeline. The editors of the volume were Edward Waldo Emerson and Waldo Emerson Forbes—one Ralph Waldo's son, the other his stepson (not especially creative with the names, this family). The brothers are chatty archivists. Throughout the text, small asides and annotations pop up—adding context, clarifying who a certain letter's recipient is and their relationship to Emerson the elder. Just before a spring entry appears, this intriguing note from the editors:

> "In the expression of doubts in the later part of the following entry, and perhaps in some allusions later, there seem to appear reflections of the writer's conversations with a new and notable friend. At St. Augustine he met Napoleon Achille Murat, eldest son of Joachim Murat, Napoleon's brilliant cavalry leader . . ."

Here, I backed up a few lines. Napoleon? Like, *the* Napoleon? French guy with the three-cornered hat? I tried to remember my middle-school Florida history, what years the state was under French control, when it was the Spanish claiming ownership. Alas, I was not usually paying much attention in class then, but I confirmed that it was indeed he of the funny hat that this new character in Emerson's journal was related to. *What a cool meeting of the minds,* I thought—this titan of American letters and this highfalutin French prince, rubbing elbows in St. Augustine, of all places. If they'd mentioned this in my Florida history class, maybe I wouldn't have been texting under my desk.

As I kept reading, excited about where this new information might take my research paper, I noticed that the language of the editor's note seemed . . . suspiciously polite. Something about the tone, the word choice, made me read a bit more slowly.

> "Emerson by chance met Murat, who was two years the elder, and the young men were drawn to one another. Murat, brave, frank and friendly, had a very active mind, but was skeptical as to religious dogmas . . . Emerson, of course, was much disturbed at the frank agnosticism of this admirable youth, and gave him his first ideas of the liberal and humane view of the Channing Unitarians."

Why was this encounter described with such vagueness, in contrast to some of the other extremely specific histories of the people Emerson met on his travels? What, exactly, did "drawn to one another" mean? I worked part-time at a bookstore, and the note read more to me like the back cover of some of the enemies-to-lovers romance novels that flew off the shelves. A smart, flamboyant, and foreign (royal!) atheist; a somber, devout American poet—someone call Nora Ephron, right? *Okay, too far,* I thought, stifling my giggles in the silent library.

Of course, historians have often used the term "friend" to cover a multitude of nuances when describing important figures of the same gender whose relationships challenge the definition of the term. I've always had a romantic imagination. I was just projecting, or reading too much into it, looking for a subtext where there wasn't one. I was not going to find some earth-shaking gay revelation about one of this country's most important writers in an office across the street from something called Blue Mermaid.

So why did I find myself digging deeper, wanting it to be there?

It seemed to me that these paragraphs were obscuring something. Call it intuition or my "gaydar" tingling as I flipped the onion-skin pages of the journals. I read on, scanning for Murat's name. It came up soon after—in another letter from Emerson to his brother, written from Charleston, South Carolina, on April 23, 1827:

"My Dear Brother—
I arrived here yesterday, after a direful passage of nine days from St. Augustine. The ordinary one is one or two days. We were becalmed, tempest-tossed, and at last well nigh starved, but the beloved brother bore it not only with equanimity, but plea-sure, for my kind genius had sent me for my ship-mate Achille Murat, the eldest son of the old King Joachim. He is now a planter at Tallahassee and at this time on his way to visit his un-cle [Joseph Bonaparte -ed.] at Bordentown. He is a philosopher, a scholar, a man of the world; very skeptical but very candid, and an ardent lover of the truth. I blessed my stars for my fine companion and we talked incessantly. Much more of him when I see you."

Well, I thought. *That settles it.* Whatever had alerted my suspicions as to a potential love interest was wishful thinking. They were just trauma-bonded! They'd experienced a hurricane together—at sea, no less. As a lifelong Floridian, I'm well aware of the friendships and community that can form when facing down gale-force winds and blinding sheets of rainwater. I'm sure the two young men gravitated toward one an-other; they were both of a privileged class, most likely separated from the crew and laborers while aboard the ship. I imagined them passing several scary hours with long conversations about faith, philosophy, their hopes and dreams. They probably talked about where one might end up after they die—maybe even an untimely death—as they looked out their porthole across the darkened skies.

After reading this tale of the two men's almost-doomed trip to Charleston, spirits slightly dampened, I found an entry in Emerson's private journal, dated two weeks before the letter written to Emerson's brother. This account of meeting Murat took a different posture.

Charleston, April 6, 1827

A new event is added to the quiet history of my life. I have connected myself by friendship to a man who with as ardent a love of truth as that which animates me, with a mind surpassing mine in the variety of its research, and sharpened and strengthened to an energy for action to which I have no pretension, by advantages of birth and practical connexion with mankind beyond almost all men in the world,—is, yet, that which I had ever supposed only a creature of the imagination—a consistent Atheist,—and a disbeliever in the existence, and of course, in the immortality of the soul. My faith in these points is strong and I trust, as I live, indestructible. Meantime I love and honour this intrepid doubter. His soul is noble, and his virtue, as the virtue of a Sadducee must always be, is sublime.

Suddenly, it was feeling pretty warm in that research library. I took some more notes, compiled what I needed for my paper, and left to wander the oldest city with a new, curious lens to look through. What did it look like—St. Augustine, two centuries ago—to a young romantic? Maybe, even, one who was falling in love?

~

Months later, I was reading about the Hotel Ponce de Leon when I came across a series of photos that jogged my memory of the day at the Lightner Museum. The first was of the entrance to the alleged Fountain of Youth, as it stood in 1914, and the other was the photo of the hotel I'd seen before, credited as a still from *A Florida Enchantment*. I remembered the strange silent movie and decided to look it up. This time, I made it past the blackface and found a whole host of wildly confusing contradictions that sent my brain into overdrive.

What started out as a typical silent film, with striking ladies and be-suited gentlemen emoting around lavish interiors, slowly evolved into one of the most transgressive films set in Florida that I've ever seen.

A young woman, Lillian, has come to Florida to visit her aunt and meet up with her fiancé Fred, ahead of their impending marriage. When she arrives, she finds that he has been flirting with the local women. They get into an impressively gesticulated fight. The next day, she visits a local curiosity shop and finds a box there, identical to one she's seen at her aunt's house, that contains a cryptic note and four seeds. The note claims that the box washed ashore, on Anastasia Island, one hundred years earlier. Its author says they shipwrecked off the coast of Africa, where they witnessed a group of natives who were able to renumber their ranks by capturing women from neighboring tribes and turning them into men.

The box at her aunt's house also contains a note that reads: "In the duplicate of this casket, whereabouts unknown, lies a secret for all women who suffer. Ha! Ha!" Lillian, still angry at her fiancé, who has ditched her again, impulsively eats one of the seeds from the twin box and heads off to bed.

The next title card reads: THE METAMORPHOSIS OF LILLIAN TRAVERS. Lillian heads to her vanity to get ready for the day, only to discover she is now sporting a thick mustache. She shaves it off, but her mannerisms have changed too. Lillian walks with a cowhand's bowed legs, punches people at random, kisses and puts her arm around the young ladies her fiancé was entertaining in the garden. She gives her maid one of the seeds too, and she starts a transformation of her own. Eventually, Lillian starts dressing as a man, changes her name to Lawrence, and leaves Florida by boat, up the Ocklawaha River. Lillian's clothes are thrown overboard, and both Lawrence and his former maid, fully transformed into passable men, step off the boat to live new lives.

Fred, who has followed his fiancée onto the boat, believes Lillian is dead after finding the abandoned clothes floating in the water and traces her disappearance to a strange man unknown to him—Lawrence. More chaos ensues, ending in Fred wearing women's clothes, transforming himself, until he is chased through historic downtown St. Augustine and the Castillo, jumps off a pier, and eventually drowns. The camera fades to black, then fades back in onto Lillian, sitting in her chair with the note from the box clutched in her hand. Fred walks in and finds her, and the final title card appears, of Lillian saying, "Oh, Fred, I've had such a horrible dream!" It was no *Sopranos* finale, but I still felt a bit disappointed.

This is the shortest possible synopsis of *A Florida Enchantment* that I can provide and still make a lick of sense. It is a *wild* film. I'm leaving out all kinds of details and plot points, and I can't, in good faith, recommend this movie. It's incredibly racist and uses harmful stereotypes of all kinds as the basis for much of its plot machinations. I think it's worth consideration, historically and symbolically, despite its many ugly features. As far as I can tell, this is the first movie in which queer and/or cross-dressing characters appear in Florida cinematic history.

There are shots of old Florida's landscapes and historic buildings that remind the viewer of the wildness of the location at the time of the film's production, how underdeveloped it is in contrast to what those cities look like today. The whole time I watched the movie, mouth agape, I was struck by how boundary-pushing it still felt, a century after it first found audiences. Amid its worst moments and cheap, slapstick laughs at the expense of Black and effeminate white male characters, there are some surprisingly progressive ideas. (While I know, of course, that things can be both queer and racist simultaneously, it's always a bit mind-melting to encounter in the wild.) Ideas, it turns out, that reinforce something I've had a nagging feeling about ever since reading about Ralph and Achille in the research library, ideas pulling at me as I wandered the Lightner Museum, that were starting to look dangerously like a theory.

Certainly, I can't be the first person to type "Ralph Waldo Emerson gay real proof" into Google's search bar. But it doesn't seem like there have been *enough* of us doing so to result in any incontrovertible evidence in either direction, true or false. My late-night searches did help me find a reference to a Harvard classmate of Emerson's, dated even earlier than the St. Augustine journals, and a poem written about that classmate—a young man named Martin Gay. Emerson writes about Gay in a passage dated August 8, 1820:

"A strange face in the Freshman class whom I should like to know very much. He has a great deal of character in his features. . . . His name is Gay. I shall endeavor to become acquainted with him & wish if possible that I might be able to recall at a future period the singular sensations which his presence produced . . ."

In another, from May of 1821:

"I am more puzzled than ever with Gay's conduct. He came out to meet me yesterday, but just before we met, I turned another corner and most strangely avoided him. This morning I went out to meet him in a different direction and stopped to speak to a lounger so as to be directly in Gay's way, but he turned into the first gate and went toward Stoughton. All this child's play persists without any apparent design, and as soberly as if both of us were intent on some tremendous affair."

Okay, come on.

I felt an instant kinship with young Ralphie and his classic teenage crush behavior. Who among us has not put themselves directly in their crush's eyeline, seemingly by accident, only to purposely avoid them the next? Heated debates about philosophy over candlelit pages can feel more like love than actual sex to some, especially those who go on to write poetry and essays taught in classrooms across the globe. Whether or not Emerson acted on these infatuations or not doesn't change the fact of their existence, and I can't think of much stronger proof than his own words. Writers tell on themselves.

It's worth noting, too, that these kinds of relationships were not unique to Emerson. Much scholarship exists on the homosocial relationships of the time, especially between the transcendentalist writers. Writer Jordan Alexander Stein explores how Melville and Hawthorne used language to allude to their desire for one another in an essay for the Los Angeles Review of Books, brazenly titled "History's Dick Jokes: On Melville and Hawthorne." In it, Stein writes about the "tantalizing" book reviews that Melville wrote and the language of his own prose that hints at these kinds of relationships. But it wasn't until I reached another passage in Stein's essay that I was able to pinpoint what I found so fascinating about Emerson and Murat:

"If then we are concerned with Melville and Hawthorne's relationship—if we believe it will tell us something about these two authors, or about American literature, or about, perhaps most compellingly, the history of desire—we have no access to that desire itself. All we are left with are representations of Melville's feelings, tantalizingly expressed without being particularly easy to pinpoint. Melville wrote of Hawthorne with undeniably sexy language. What proves more elusive are the feelings to which, with any precision, this language can be said to refer."

I wonder, as I contemplate Emerson, if I feel frustrated by that lack of "access to that desire itself." Desire is, as Stein says, difficult to locate; it's one of those know-it-when-you-see-it kinds of things. Was this prose accidentally sexy? Or meant to serve as a beacon to other writers in a time when they were all closely reading one another's work, across many miles and beaches and stormy seas? Was there a code being developed?

I kept thinking about Emerson and Murat. I realized that rather than wanting to find out the truth of their relationship, regardless of the outcome, like a good researcher would, I *really wanted* Emerson to be gay. Like, certifiably. Why did I feel this way? Why such a strong desire for clear, incontrovertible "proof"?

Besides, what does "proof" of queerness even look like? That is extremely tricky territory, especially in a world that still treats bisexuality as a myth or a novelty; that legislates gender expression through a rigid concept of external anatomy; that denies the existence of many in-between, nonbinary, or overlapping aspects of queer identity. What would count as "proof" of any one person's queerness in the twenty-first century, let alone that of one in 1827? What would make me say, "Yes, that's it, I knew it!"? A play-by-play account of a confirmed tryst, hastily scrawled by candlelight and stashed somewhere? A journal page somehow tucked beneath another, overlooked for a century, that reads, "Dear Brother, today I kissed Achille Murat right on his beautiful French mouth"?

I worry about crossing a boundary. A poet who visited my graduate course, one who has herself done some writing that posthumously "queers" a historical figure, tells me to be careful making claims about Emerson.

"He's one of the big boys," she says. "No one cared what I was doing because no one had ever heard of who I was writing about. But you might get pushback."

~

A recent auction took place, in which the personal effects of writer Joan Didion were sold online. I perused the collection with a lusty eye and a threadbare wallet. I adore Didion, and something appealed to me about having some kind of sacred relic that once belonged to her in my possession. But as I watched the bids skyrocket, including for a stack of blank, untouched, otherwise unmemorable Moleskines that were going for around $1,200 apiece, I wondered what exactly made these objects worth such ridiculous sums.

In part, I think Didion's particular brand aligns itself with beautiful material things, like her famous Celine sunglasses. Emerson's legacy is decidedly more . . . utilitarian, if not any less prestigious. His esteemed artifacts are books, journals, maybe a dusty old cravat behind glass in someone's private collection. Emerson's legacy is in no real danger of being sold off, part and parcel, to a marketing director in Park Slope. But I worry about making any kind of claims about his identity all the same. Would people be angry? His descendants, school boards, tenured professors with liver-spotted hands and an attachment to American masculinity? I wonder about who gets to own a part of a writer, either materially or existentially.

Even in Emerson's day, the transient nature of so many of the people living in Florida at any given time likely shaped their conception of themselves as visitors or people in an in-between place. Perhaps Emerson's visit was actually the inciting incident of his creative life. Whether his relationship with Murat—borne of a scary evening at sea, discussing life and death and fate in a cramped cabin—eventually became romantic? It might be beside the point.

The real reason I'm so fascinated with this discovery isn't actually that Ralph Waldo Emerson may have been gay. It's that he may have been gay *in Florida*. I feel a sense of pride, no pun intended, when I let myself believe it. That he might have felt his most authentic self on our shores. It's the same glimmering feeling I get every summer in St. Petersburg, home of the largest LGBTQ Pride parade in Florida, as our city opens its arms to thousands of visitors. It's there, in thinking that a movie as unabashedly queer as *A Florida Enchantment* is one of our oldest contributions to cinema.

Consider the long lineage of queer Florida writers, known or unknown. Tennessee Williams, not a born-and-raised Floridian, but one who lived here for thirty-four years, considered the Keys the closest thing to home he'd had. Dozens of Williams's famous friends, among them Truman Capote, visited him here, escaping some of the tighter strictures of homophobia in their more "civilized" residences of New York or Los Angeles in the forties. Williams found more freedom in Florida to live as he wanted, and his best work was made in the tropical heat.

Elizabeth Bishop's house is now home to a yearly literary festival in the Keys. Hemingway, held up by so many as an icon of straight American masculinity, wrote some of his gayest books (if you ask me) while he lived in Florida, including *The Garden of Eden,* which is an incredibly nuanced look at gender dysphoria, cross-dressing, and queer desire. (It's worth noting that it was released posthumously.) We get to claim Rita Mae Brown, whose autobiographical novel *Rubyfruit Jungle* is gloriously queer—and gloriously Floridian too.

The list goes on and on: Andrew Holleran's hauntingly beautiful novels of north Florida, Kristen Arnett's messy lesbians flailing and flirting in Orlando, Jaquira Díaz's tough and tender Miami girls. Edgar Gomez writes love letters to his immigrant Florida family and the Latinx queer community, as well as heartfelt elegies for Pulse victims. Richard Blanco and Tyler Gillespie put this place into every line of their poems, and we are better readers because they do. Dozens, hundreds, hopefully thousands of queer writers whose names we don't know yet. Floridians are spoiled for queer artists. The problematic parts of this place have always existed, of course, but running right alongside them is a liberatory streak as long and beautiful—and as threatened—as our coastline.

The only proof I have of Emerson's queerness is my intuition, a hunch. I also have my understanding of St. Augustine, of Florida, and its location at the intersection of so many aspects of history, literature, politics, and American identity. Emerson was so young when he was in St. Augustine—newly freed from school, ill but not debilitated, no job, no responsibilities to speak of. No one who knew him from home, no reputation to live up to—at least not yet. I imagine him wandering the narrow alleys of the old town, hands in his pockets, looking into windows and through café doors. In existing in this liminal space, with ample boredom, an overactive mind, and all kinds of new people, I wonder if the boundaries of his "real" life started to smudge and blur.

As Emerson himself says, he had never even imagined a creature like Murat—a thinking, empathetic atheist, his intellectual match and simultaneous foil. Maybe they didn't swap spit, per se. I'm willing to leave that door ajar until further notice. But they certainly swapped ideas—shared their hopes and dreams on a wild, turbulent expanse of water just adjacent to a place undergoing a rapid transformation of its own. I imagine that young man, rolling his orange the same way I roll these thoughts along in my own head as I drive south, back home to the Gulf shores of Tampa Bay, pelicans and sandhill cranes crossing the bridge back to the mainland above and alongside my car. The statues of lions and the limestone of the fort recede behind me, blurring and shrinking as the setting sun makes me shield my eyes.

St. Augustine is ancient and modern and sacred and weird. I came back there after a long time away, in New York City—a place that gave me the same freedom so many seek when they come to Florida. In New York, away from my religious background and the people who knew me when I was young, I could be whatever version of myself I wanted to be on any given day. But only once I returned, when I started to seek out the history of my own home and found so much hidden under the limestone, did I realize I never needed to leave. It was already here. I think this as I drive through the wild swamp, containing within its state lines the oldest site of American multicultural exchange, built definitively into our nation's history, hinted at in the pages of journals and the backgrounds of paintings and in books yet to be printed. Florida is, and always has been, a queer place.

agua mala

My phone chimed:

"i'm outside."

I looked up from the text screen and peeked through the blinds to see Mikey's truck idling in the alley. It was 2011, and I was in St. Petersburg, Florida, at my parents' house, visiting for the weekend. I walked across the linoleum with my shoes in my hand, as softly as I could. The drone of my dad's box fan drowned out any noise made by the opening and shutting of the side door, but I did it gently anyway. Old habits die hard.

I didn't live there anymore, and I was a grown woman—or at least I thought I was. I was at least half-grown, I told myself at the age of twenty-three. I was under no one's jurisdiction but my own. I could do what I wanted, but I didn't really know what that meant yet.

Still, I was careful and light-footed as I followed my old escape route like muscle memory. I'd done that walk many times when I was in high school, and the steps were familiar. I balanced on the balls of my bare feet across the gravel driveway toward the black F-150, the same place where Mikey once convinced my little brothers he could turn the truck into a jet at a moment's notice. I opened the high passenger-side door and swung myself up and in, brushing little pieces of rock off my feet before shutting the door behind me. Mikey gave me that familiar boy-nod, an almost indiscernible raise of his chin, and set down his phone. His soft brown curls scraped the top of the truck's cloth interior as he leaned forward to shift into drive.

It had been at least a year since I'd seen him, maybe more. Mikey wasn't visiting home—he lived there again. He moved back after barely finishing undergrad at Florida State, a short drive north from Gainesville, where I lived the rest of the year. I didn't know what he was doing now, if he was working or not, how he spent most of his time. That's why he picked me up, ostensibly—to "catch up." Our eyes met in the rearview mirror's reflection.

"Shadrack's?"

I nodded or made some noise of affirmation, holding his gaze for longer than I should have. He looked the same; he was just bigger somehow. Taking up more space. Or maybe I just wanted it to be that way, my arm on the center console, the two of us a little closer to touching than not. He pulled out of the alley quietly, slowly, and waited until we were on the main road to the beach before he turned the radio up. He was listening to Young Jeezy. Both of these facts—the song, the turning it down before pulling up—made me smile. More old habits.

I looked out across the water as we came to a stop at the bridge light and squinted, trying to find Mosquito Island in the dark. I hadn't been out there since our senior year of high school, a graduation keg party, I think. I pointed at a dark smudge in the Gulf, a vacuum where no dock lights showed through, and asked him if that was right. He craned a thick eyebrow and looked at me sideways.

"Mosquito Island is on the other side of the Don from here," he said.

I flushed. We were miles away from where I thought we were. I'd been gone longer than I realized, and it smelled like it was about to rain, so I rolled up the window.

~

Midway through the sixth season of *The X-Files,* FBI agents Fox Mulder and Dana Scully find themselves in the town of Goodland, Florida. They are there at the behest of retired agent Arthur Dales, who has received a distressing call from a neighbor concerning her husband's disappearance. Dales suspects paranormal activity. Mulder agrees. Scully is eager to prove them both wrong.

During Mulder and Scully's stay in Goodland, a storm—Hurricane Leroy—makes landfall. The agents track Dales down to his mobile home, drenched and windblown from the first of Leroy's feeder bands making landfall. The neighbor describes her husband's attacker as "something with tentacles." Dales suggests the culprit is a violent sea creature. Ever our skeptic, spotting several empty whiskey bottles in the trash, Scully is dismissive of such murky logic. Her hair is soaking wet and drips into her eyes. She rolls those big green eyes and pulls up the hood of her raincoat, turning to leave.

"Don't sneer at the mysteries of the deep, young lady," Dales warns her, leering ominously while lightning flashes. "The bottom of the ocean is as deep and dark as the imagination."

With that, our two heroes venture out into the worsening storm, trailer door flailing wildly behind them. They make a mismatched pair: one eager, one reluctant, in search of some lethal, many-limbed beast.

~

In 2016, the Delray Beach Fire Department added a grief counselor to their payroll. Firefighters and EMTs had borne witness to so many deaths by opioid overdose that their supervisors were noting a "callousness" toward victims, a pattern of dehumanizing. This kind of behavior is a common early warning sign of post-traumatic stress disorder, as the brain struggles to process overwhelming amounts of grief.

One opioid in particular—fentanyl—is responsible for the majority of the overdose deaths in South Florida. A 2021 report prepared by Project Opioid Tampa Bay states that three people die every hour from opioid-related causes. For the first time since the 1910s, life expectancy in our state has dropped. This problem isn't unique to Florida, but it's especially virulent here; it can feel, at times, like the drug is seeping into the limestone under our feet.

Fentanyl is an anesthetic, roughly fifty to a hundred times stronger than morphine. It was developed for the management of severe, chronic pain caused by aggressive terminal cancer treatments, but it quickly escaped containment, finding its way into dubiously licensed doctor's offices and the hands of street dealers. Fentanyl is sneaky, lethal in small doses, and hard to detect when cut into other drugs like cocaine or prescription opiates. Anyone who was a young person in Florida in the 2000s can attest to these drugs' ease of access—oxys, roxys, percs, whatever. Someone knew someone who always had them available. To me, the proliferation of fentanyl seems like the sadly logical next step in a chain of events that have made opiates as much a part of the Florida ecosystem as lionfish or kudzu.

The state and federal governments' response to this wave of opioid addiction has been confusing. As recently as 2016, the Drug Enforcement Administration (DEA) alleged incidences of contact overdose in a training video and encouraged first responders not to touch overdosed patients without gloves. (The video, and any mention of it on the DEA's website, no longer exists.) There have been no scientific studies that prove this skin-to-skin contagion to be true, but the messaging is familiar; it's straight out of the AIDS playbook. If you render a victim untouchable, make their affliction one of moral consequences and not material circumstances, the true monster can lurk beneath the surface a while longer, undisturbed.

Even when they seek help, people addicted to opioids aren't out of Florida's tangled net just yet. Treatment centers in South Florida have gained a dubious reputation for a handful of reasons. These for-profit clinics incentivize the prolonged illness of their patients. Florida rehab centers often analyze the urine of their patients for signs of relapse. The patient's insurance is then billed for the cost of these tests. The more frequent the testing, the more money the center can collect. In an investigation conducted by the *New York Times,* one patient's mother reported a charge to her insurance of $9,500 for five urinalysis tests, and twenty-one such tests in one year.

Another slimy phenomenon is "body brokering," in which recovering addicts can receive treatments from facilities but live off-property in "sober homes," privately owned halfway houses (whose owners are often given illegal kickbacks from the urinalysis profits that the rehab centers rake in). The rehab centers refer their discharged patients to these sober houses for probationary periods designated by law enforcement or family services.

Eric Snyder, one operator of a rehab treatment center and halfway house in Delray Beach, was charged with fraudulent urinalysis billing of $58.2 million in 2019. According to the complaint, Snyder and associates "trolled AA meetings and 'crack motels' to find patients." Urine samples were double-billed and split into multiple test samples to maximize submissions. Facility employees who target addicts for treatment are referred to in-house as "junkie hunters." Upon re-entry to facilities, insurance benefits are reset, and the cycle repeats.

The language of addiction response is always, intentionally, maddeningly, vague. It fails to address the specificities of the problem. "Crisis" avails the monster of a discernible face but gives it a moral center. "Epidemic" implies a vast, sweeping wave, its point of origin somewhere far offshore. It shields those who stand to profit off addiction from culpability. According to the state's Surgeon General, ninety of the top one hundred physicians across the country who purchased and prescribed oxycodone in the last ten years did so in Florida.

Doctors, rehab centers, and for-profit "sober houses" are shielded by language too. They serve "junkies," not patients. Their offices are "pill mills," even while they advertise, full-page and full-color, in award-winning newspapers. Their faces loom, twenty feet tall and spotlit, on billboards along I-95—next to signs hawking iguana removal services and informing tourists of the approaching casino exit. Addiction is woven into the fabric of life here; it's just something you live with, holding your nose, like red tide creeping closer and closer to the mainland every year.

Addicts in Florida are kept in a stranglehold; the sticky limbs of money, incarceration, healthcare, and exploitation intertwined. The sicker the patient, the more profit can be drained from their increasingly compromised veins. One tentacle is cut off and five more grow back in its place.

When I was a kid, there was a common saying: "Come on vacation, leave on probation." In the forementioned *X-Files* episode "Agua Mala," the local deputy pulls a gun on Mulder and Scully. When they tell him they're FBI, he says, "Well. Don't all the nuts roll down to Florida?"

These jokes work on the surface, from a sense of distant wonder. But they also serve another, more insidious purpose. Linguistically, they traffic well-worn roads. Vulgarity, unseriousness, dismissal. Low-hanging citrus. Reduce the state to a punchline and you no longer have to engage with the very real dangers facing the very real human beings who live there.

~

I ran into a ghost a few weeks after moving back to Florida from New York, in the fall of 2020. An old friend of mine, Charlotte, was a hair stylist now, and I was waiting my turn to see her when I locked eyes with my other old friend, Sam. His long hair was slightly damp, but he wore it in the same style as when we were kids. He recognized me, then quickly looked away, but I waved, forcing him to acknowledge me. We exchanged pleasantries, then I asked him how Mikey had been, and he stiffened. Gently, he deflected the conversation and said we should get a beer some time. He had to run.

I was confused. Sam and Mikey had been like brothers since the day I met them. Asking Sam about him felt like muscle memory. When I got to Charlotte's chair, I asked her what that was all about, why he'd acted so weird.

"Riiiiight," she said, winding my hair up from the nape of my neck and clipping it. She draped the plastic cape around my shoulders and snapped it shut, looking at my reflection's eyes as she often did. "You don't know?"

Something hot and salty surged in my chest. I didn't know. But I knew.

~

One of my favorite things about *The X-Files* (and there are so many gifts the show gave us; Google 'Gillian Anderson Vanity Fair Party outfit' if you love yourself) is the way the show plays Fox and Dana against one another, the believer and the doubter, to keep the audience always suspended on the edge of certainty. "Spooky" Mulder operates from the standpoint that the supernatural is real, all around us, that conspiracy theories can explain all kinds of bizarre activity.

He "wants to believe." Scully, rational and methodical, prefers to rely on evidence and fieldwork when confronted with the inexplicable. She operates from the skeptical end of the spectrum, that other famous tagline attributed to the show: "The truth is out there."

Interestingly, Agent Scully is a lapsed Catholic. Although she believes in science, she often cites the concept of having faith in the unknown to Mulder whenever a religious element comes into play in a case. Her malleability in this aspect keeps their dynamic clear of the one-note, buddy-cop style of writing that might otherwise bore this viewer. Dozens of Reddit threads have been devoted to fans' frustration with Scully, that even after several seasons of close encounters with monsters, G-men, and extraterrestrials, she still doesn't believe.

Late in the first season, a notable episode, "Beyond the Sea," has Mulder and Scully essentially swap roles. A killer who looks a lot like The Night Stalker, Richard Ramirez, seems to have psychic abilities. Scully has just lost her father to a heart attack, and when the killer uses things her father has said to her to mess with her head, the lines get blurred and the walls she's built against such tactics are much more permeable. All of a sudden, she has reason to believe.

~

I always find myself saying that Mikey and I lost touch "after high school," but that's not the truth. Mikey and I became friends in the first place *during* high school, yes, after a moment of mutual recognition. We had English class together. Mikey was a tall, handsome, basketball-playing social butterfly, part of a group of boys who called themselves "ATK." It stood for something different depending on who you asked, but the most common answer was "Alpha Tappa Kegga," a fictional fraternity of bronzed boys who threw parties on sandbars and the barrier islands around our beach town, arriving on their parents' borrowed boats. I was a former cheerleader turned wannabe riot girl, always at shows in church basements and punk houses and coffee shops, the budding of a Tampa alternative music scene happening just when I needed it.

We met one another in our freshman English class. Me, still blonde, Jesus-loving; him deep-voiced even then, Star of David pendant glinting against his polo shirt. We were assigned to a group project, working together on a presentation about *Brave New World.* We circled one another like sharks at first, until we each saw something we recognized and locked steps. I realize now that maybe we saw each other at first because we were both impossibly sad. I don't mean "impossible" in the sense that our sadness was so deep or vast that it was unknowable; I mean that by looking at either of us then, you'd never have guessed that we were drowning. We each had plenty of friends, seemingly supportive families, and siblings who played sports. What did we have to be depressed about?

In a photo I have, we are sitting on a couch in that English classroom. On the far left is my friend Ally, who went to Jewish day school with Mikey. She's flashing a peace sign. Mikey's right arm is around her, his curly hair propping up a baseball hat, part of his Billabong sweatshirt visible. He is making a weird, pursed-lip smirking face, the kind boys made in pictures then to keep from smiling and looking uncool. His other arm is around my shoulder, not actually touching it but hovering a few inches above it. My knees are pulled up into my lap, and I'm leaning in toward him. On my other side, smiling like he knows exactly what's happening here, is Sam. It's just a photo, taken on an ancient digital camera, but I see it for what I remember feeling the moment it was taken: an excuse to be close to each other.

Mikey and I were still close friends in college, talking on the phone basically every other night, even though he moved to Tallahassee, and I ended up first in Orlando, then Gainesville, then eventually New

York. We talked consistently, if not constantly. I always knew what he was up to. Our tentative high school feelings toward one another ebbed and flowed—sometimes romantic, sometimes not, depending on the severity of each of our mental illnesses and whether or not we were dating anyone. We'd stay up on Skype until the sun came up one weekend, then not speak for six months. He met a girl at a party, or his ex, Becca, was single again and ready to reconcile. I knew I was never his first choice, and maybe he wasn't mine either, but the thrum of our connection to one another never went dead. We would expand on contact, make room for each other in our lives without hesitation, fall back into our old rhythms, until we didn't anymore.

I took one ill-fated trip to a frat party in Tallahassee one Halloween when Mikey and I still lived a few hours away from each other. He was in an off-campus apartment with black mold in Tallahassee, and I lived with my sister in a condo in Gainesville while I tried, desperately, to reinvent myself as an adult. All of my other friends were going, and even though things between Mikey and I were weird, I wouldn't pass up a chance to see him, so I hitched a ride. When we got there, the party was already in full swing. Mikey was dressed as The Bear Jew, a character from the movie *Inglourious Basterds* who wore an A-line tank top and carried a bloodied baseball bat that he'd used to kill Nazis in the movie.

At our public high school, Mikey had been a constant recipient of teasing as one of the few visibly Jewish kids there. His newfound college-gym muscle mass and pride at seeing a hero like The Bear Jew on-screen (plus, probably, several funnels of beer that night) gave him a giddiness that bordered on violence. I was a Rockford Peach and also carried a baseball bat, although it was plastic; we took pictures together at an imaginary home plate. The party went on. A few games of beer pong loosened our limbs, and eventually, the partygoers dwindled. I'd been through a recent breakup and felt like maybe the universe had led me there, to the boy who knew all my tender places and still liked me. It never really occurred to me that he might be covering his own sadness with layers of Jägermeister and a part-time job making pizzas.

Eventually, I realized that the friends I'd carpooled with had left without me to go on a Tally bar crawl. It was too loud in the living room to sleep on the couch, but if I didn't get horizontal soon, there would be neon-orange Sparks barf on my polyester costume. I managed to yell a few words into Mikey's eardrum, however coherent, and he excused himself from beer pong to attend to my crisis. He got fresh sheets and blankets from somewhere and made me a space in his bed, rifling through his drawers for basketball shorts and a T-shirt while I laid in a daze and stared up at his *Goodfellas* poster, wondering if he might be my soulmate.

After I'd wrangled my unresponsive limbs into his giant clothes, I came back to bed to find him sitting on it with four Advil, a Gatorade, and his phone set up on the nightstand. He'd loaded up a long YouTube clip of Stevie Nicks singing "Wild Heart" backstage at a concert in the seventies, one of my favorite things to watch. I tried to ask him how he knew about it, muckle-mouthed and lazy-eyed, looking, I'm sure, like a total mess. Gently, he took my socks off. I tried to kiss him, groped wildly at his basketball shorts. He moved out of reach without comment and held out the Gatorade, watching closely to make sure I finished it. I asked again how he knew about the video, how he knew to show it to me now, as if it were some rare artifact.

"Because you've sent it to me, like, ten times," Mikey said, pulling lightly on my earlobe as I groaned and nuzzled into the pillow. How embarrassing. He turned out the light, and I fell, almost immediately, asleep. When I woke up the next morning, my head felt split in half. I woke up with his hand in mine, at an odd angle. He had eventually settled onto a pile of blankets on the floor of his own bedroom, arm raised above his head to rest on the edge of the mattress the whole night.

We all went to Denny's, then my friends and I drove back to Gainesville. I spent the whole ride thinking about the distance between our bodies the night before and what it meant that Mikey had let that space stay peacefully unconquered. That was not always the way it was, at other parties, with other boys. I was grateful for the bone-deep faith I had, breathing into his sweaty pillow, that I was safe. He always seemed to know before I did when we were getting into murky waters, when we were trying to force things or make whatever this unnamable thing between us was into a defined territory. Over the following years, we took turns reinforcing the borders of the space between us—sometimes with resistance, sometimes with mutual absence. I finally buried the part of me that had dangled a hand over the bed all night, grateful I'd been given the gift of someone who saw me, at least, and didn't run away. Bolstered by that recognition, I eventually took a chance and left the place where we were from—left him—behind.

It was gradual at first. Missed emails. Phone tag back and forth. Weeks, a month. This was our way, but one day, I felt a weird persistence of uneasiness, an unmistakable absence. I tried calling on lunch breaks and subway rides, but the number I always called was disconnected. Sometimes a message from T-Mobile would auto-play. It was one I recognized, from when I'd first moved to the city and had trouble paying my own bill. My emails to Mikey went unanswered for months at a time, only to be answered at random with a long, confusing apology that sounded like it was written after a few beers.

It didn't concern me. By then, I was so far away. It almost felt like a relief not to have to start the conversations, which were always over the phone. They lasted a long time and derailed my plans. We had trouble hanging up. It was part of the dance, I told myself. Mikey had ghosted on and off the entirety of our friendship. We both tended to sink inside ourselves when the veil of our depressions started to descend, and we always knew it wasn't personal. Mikey would sometimes lock his phone in a drawer. The mounting voicemails made it worse. He always showed up eventually. It's just the way he is. Or was. I'm not sure.

It's hard to tell when a pattern becomes a trend, becomes a fact. I was in New York. I told myself I was busy becoming something, the writer we'd both wanted me to become. He was still in Florida. Our friendship felt disjointed, a tin can on the other end of a string. I put it out of mind. I worked and wrote, went back to school, built a wall in my memory between the now and the then—a swampy void that, if I thought about it for too long, might launch me onto an airplane and back into the muck of the past.

Eventually, I did become something, that someone, I guess. Older. Someone with someone else to think about. I fell in love, got engaged. I tried to track down Mikey's address to send him an invitation to my wedding that fall. Still nothing. Finally, I pasted the date and details into a Facebook message, the last bastion of communication he seemed able to access. Silence.

Then, about two weeks before the wedding, a message: "sorry. i'll be there. prolly gonna ride up with sam and brianna. wouldn't miss it."

Sure enough, there he was, in 2017, on my wedding day. All six feet, four inches of him in a beige suit, sitting at the end of a wooden bench on one side of Brianna, in her long floral dress and curls blowing in the breeze. Sam, Mikey's best friend, sat on her other side, smirking, never not goofing off.

In the wild, watercolor smudge of my memories from that day, the three of them on that bench are sharp. I remember locking eyes with them while I made my way down the middle of the crowd. Mostly, I remember Mikey after the ceremony. I caught a glimpse of him from far away while talking to someone, and had to squint to figure out who it was. Perpetually scowling until he settled in, slouching a little. He had always looked and sounded way older than he was when we were younger, until you made him laugh, when the furrow between his brows and his high, tanned cheekbones smoothed out into a solid plane. He'd bulked up—puffy-cheeked, bleary-eyed, no longer scrawny, but still so tall. I barely had time to talk to him in the madness of the day, but I stopped at their table during dinner to say hi and thank them for coming. When I got to the table, Mikey stood from his chair and lifted me up into a tight hug, careful not to smash my hair down.

"You look so happy, Rach," he said. I pulled back to look at him and told him that I was. His smile was tight. That was the last time I would ever see his face.

Someone called my name. I apologized and said I had to go. I thanked him for coming, and then I walked away.

In *X-Files* lore, it's a part of Scully's background that her favorite book is *Moby Dick*. Scully's dad, the one whose death makes her believe, was a Navy captain who affectionately called her "Starbuck." I've never been able to make it through more than a chapter or two of *Moby Dick*, lost in all the intense language and impenetrable (to me) male characters. But I also have a stubborn reason for not giving it a full chance: for many years, before I moved away, my closest friends referred to Mikey as my "white whale." A simplification, I felt, of the byzantine maze I'd constructed inside of my feelings—and it sounded a little desperate. I wasn't some crazed sea captain, obsessed with finding the object of my soul's essential mythology. We were just friends.

Scully, though, seems like exactly the kind of person who would love *Moby Dick*. She has an obsession of her own—the truth—and finds herself challenged over and over again along the way. In her Salon. com essay "Scully Have I Loved," writer Rebecca Traister explains why she finds Dana Scully the more compelling half of the *X-Files* duo: "The very fact that her character was such a hard sell made her repeated brushes with the supernatural all the more powerful . . . Scully's surety was solid, stable, rigid; every time she saw something she thought she'd never see, we saw it crack, sparks fly from it." The part of Scully that I connect to is this part, the doubter who won't admit to themselves that the hard stance they've taken might be wrong. To admit that a certain future you've been chasing might actually be a figment of your imagination is more dangerous to your health than any lurking creature.

"Agua Mala" is an episode of *The X-Files* that falls under a fan-coined category: "Monster of the Week" episodes. They function as stand-alones, easy to watch with no context, a little break from the main storyline of the show, in which Mulder and Scully work against a far-reaching government conspiracy. Monster of the Week episodes gained cult status with fans as a place where the wilder, weirder regions of the paranormal could be explored without altering the timeline or events of the show in any real way. I always liked these episodes because of the narrative potential—the writers could have fun, put these two in freaky situations, and see the possibilities. By the end of the hour, the looming threat was explained away, a wrong number or misplaced shadow proving Scully right—no monsters here, just a waste of our time, a diversion.

More and more, Florida feels like a badly written Monster of the Week plot. A shadowy figure around the corner, with its mask ripped off, is revealed to be the elderly janitor from earlier, to the giggles and high-fives of the meddling kids. The episode ends, the moviegoers leave the theater, and then what? If this crisis is a monster, it is less like Freddy Krueger existing in dreamspace and more like Michael

Myers. Inevitable, unkillable, returning over and over because the townspeople think if he's out of sight, if they don't see him, he's gone. He never is.

I wish there was an ending to this case, but there isn't, even now, as I write this. The longer I've been back in my hometown, the more I run into people who knew me and Mikey both. But I don't get any more answers. The more I try to figure out why everyone is being weird, the more confused I end up. I am trying to understand something that seems like it does not want to be understood. I get more concerned the more people shy away from what I feel are casual questions. It seems like something is seriously wrong. *I just saw him,* I think, bewildered, until I do the math and realize it's been years since my wedding day.

I've headed up my own investigation, of a sort. I piece together a timeline, trying to ask the right questions of mutual friends after we've shared a beer or two, without upsetting them. It's harder work than it seems. People are angry. From what I can tell, Mikey's depression got worse. At some point after college, it evolved until he was finally diagnosed with schizophrenia after increased bouts of paranoia. His accusations caused estrangement from his family members and closest friends. He was on medication intermittently. After a few years of tough breaks, losing jobs and struggling to keep his head above water, he either totally ran out of meds or health insurance or couldn't afford them anymore. Allegedly, he started doing other drugs. Was he trying to quell the noise? Pass time? I don't know because no one wants to talk about it.

Our mutual friend, Greg, told me that he took Mikey out for a beer a while back, having finally run into him after weeks of being ghosted. Greg said when he got back from a trip to the bathroom, Mikey was talking to himself at the bar. When Greg tried to shake him out of it, he got aggressive. From what I can tell, Sam did everything he could for him—lent him money, let him crash with him—until he couldn't anymore. Angrily, I asked Greg why no one seemed to care. How could they call themselves his friend but let him slip into the cracks like that? Greg matched my anger.

"You actually don't know what the fuck you're talking about, Rachel," he said, ashing his cigarette, glaring at me. I'd known him just as long as I'd known Mikey and still saw a flicker of his teenage face under his beard. We looked at each other for a long minute, and I took another sip of my beer.

"You weren't here," Greg said.

Alone, I combed the police logs and incident reports. Medical records are private, so that was a dead end. I drove around town, past Shadrack's and the gas station that sold hot Takis and the park next to the Science Center where Mikey and I shared joints and talked about our futures. I heard from a friend of a friend that they saw him asking for money near the CVS on Fifty-Eighth, so I started going there every time I needed paper towels or face wash. Sometimes I drove by when I got hit with that salty feeling again, like a sledgehammer in my chest, sick at the thought of not knowing where he is. *If* he is. I got the feeling that a strange tide was perpetually pulling us toward and away from one another. Sometimes I'd think I see him, but when I got closer, it was a stranger.

I ran into Marcus, the older kid who always hung around our high school parties, selling everyone pills. I cornered him in the hallway of the bar and asked him if he'd seen Mikey. He said he hadn't, not in at least a year, and that was at Mastry's in the daytime so, you know. *No, I don't know. Tell me.* He said Greg made him swear not to sell to Mikey or he'd kill him. He told me he'd stuck to his promise, but you can't bullshit a bullshitter. I walked away from Marcus, back to the bar and my sweaty beer and my worry. I drifted back into a smudgy vacuum of memory, where a light should be but wasn't.

~

Toward the end of "Agua Mala," it's discovered that the monster of the week can be defeated with fresh water. It's some gloopy, nebulous creature that washed into the sewer system with the wind and rain from the hurricane, and a few quick moves from Mulder and Scully save the day. Our heroes head back to Washington to continue their hunt for the truth, which is, as the credits keep reminding us, "out there." The residents of Goodland, Florida, seemingly cease to exist.

The episode is campy, weird, and incredibly wet. It doesn't rank very high on lists of fan favorite Monsters of the Week, appearing well below glowing insects and a hybrid humanoid-fluke-worm creature. The main appeal of these episodes is how they function as a diversion: a brief, wacky respite from the "real" trouble of the story, forgotten as soon as the screen fades to black.

~

Once, we went to the beach after a few beers, me and Mikey and Sam and Brianna. We'd all had a lot to drink, and Brianna wanted to swim. The city was dredging the beach, and giant sandbags lined the shore, tarp-covered mountains standing four or five feet high. Mikey and Brianna went straight to the water, but I needed help getting over the sandbags and had to take my heels off to climb them. On the way down, I edged my bare feet across first, not realizing there were barnacles all over the side of the bags where they met the water. I sliced my right foot on one, from right between my big and second toes all the way to the middle of my sole. Sam wrapped my bleeding foot in his Guy Harvey T-shirt and called for Mikey and Brianna to come back.

When Mikey came out of the water and saw my tied-up foot, he laughed, shook his head, and knelt down so I could climb onto his back. He carried me back to the truck that way, stumbling in the sand every few steps, sending me careening precariously over his shoulder, then bouncing back into the crook of his elbows. He wasn't a seaworthy vessel, but I had no control over where we went and I couldn't walk on my own, so I just hung on, leaned my head into the space between his shoulder and neck, got quiet, and he did too, his laughter fading into a steady, rhythmic breathing that matched his trek across the beach to the parking lot, bathed in amber streetlight.

～

"Agua Mala" is also a name for the Portuguese man o' war jellyfish, most commonly used by Spanish-speaking Floridians and Caribbean islanders. The man o' war is one of the deadliest creatures to inhabit the Gulf Coast. They are driven onto beaches and bays by strong winds, especially after storms and hurricanes. It is not a true jellyfish, however; the agua mala is what is known as a siphonophore. Siphonophores are colonial creatures, made up of thousands of smaller individual organisms working together and inextricable from one another. They can partially detach from the main organism and attack, then recombine and continue to travel. They can attack while beached, while seemingly dead. It's easy to understand why some people have a fear of the ocean—like Dales tells Scully, the mysteries of the deep are terrifying. It's a place where creatures known and unknown lurk, hidden from our perception, where no light gets in, and our bodies can't survive.

But the agua mala scares me much more because it lives where we believe we are safe from threats—floating placidly on the surface, easily mistaken for a plastic bag. The things that scare me about the ocean are on the surface and the shore, like the agua mala. Like the razor-wire edge of the barnacle that cut my foot open the night Mikey carried me back to the car. Like the fact that a boy you sat next to for dozens of sunsets, who you kissed with saltwater lapping at your shoulders, whose future felt braided to your own, can disappear into broad daylight. Like a couple of granules of a synthetic substance that looks like sugar but snuffs out a life in seconds.

All of my theories about Mikey fall apart on closer inspection. It's not UFOs or fluke worms killing millions of Floridians, wrecking their lives, robbing them of jobs and families and futures. Scully taught me better; it's usually the least outlandish explanation. If you flood a state with drugs and take away all its mental health resources, people who are dependent on chemicals to live "normal" lives will seek out substitutes, however dangerous. To quiet the poison in their brains, people you love will do unexplainable things. It doesn't make them monsters. It makes them human.

My friend Ally, the girl from the high-school photo on the couch, came into my work one day when I was deep in my investigation. I told her who I'd been searching for, and her face fell.

She told me that she set him up at a halfway house, a nonprofit her mom runs. He was kicked out for stealing from other residents. She said she had seen him walking around an area just a few blocks from my house. She said that if I saw him, I could probably say hello. He might recognize me, might not. She warned me not to let him into my car or house.

"I know you loved him, Rachel," she said, "but you have to act like he's dead. For all intents and purposes, he is. The person you know is gone."

I see him now, occasionally. Circling the block near Williams Park.

Through the window, the one that looks onto the street from the corner of a dive bar I frequent. I have to admit to myself that I frequent it more often on the off chance that I might see him. Setting eyes on him feels like worrying a stone, pulling a pendant on a chain for comfort. It doesn't accomplish anything, but it still makes me feel a measure of reassurance to see some proof of life. He looks the same, but of course, he doesn't.

One time, feeling brave, I tried to get his attention, calling his name as he turned the corner. What would I have even said to him had he heard? "Hi, I miss you. I'm worried. I love you. No, wait, sorry, I *loved* you." Do I know him in past, present, or future tense? Which one makes him real? The boy I knew, the young man I left, the grown person who could have been but that I am looking at, who also isn't really him? It seems obvious that I will never know, and that my only option is to accept not knowing.

The agua mala's danger lies not just in its deadly venom, but in its method of attack, its ability to branch out unrestrained, to coil and reel in and wrap around. It has no discernible face and few known predators. No amount of superstition or logic, respectively, ensures it will not reach our shores. I watch, and I wait, looking out my passenger-side window for something once solid, now amorphous, floating just beyond my reach. I know the truth is out there, but I'm not ready. I don't want to believe.

deserter

The story of Hagar, in the Western version of the Bible, goes something like this:

Hagar is Egyptian. She is Abraham and Sarah's servant, except they are called Abram and Sarai at this point. They haven't been given their new names just yet, and Hagar is called servant, not slave. The verbiage here, as everywhere in the Bible, is important. Sarai can't have children; in Hebrew, her language, she is *akara*—barren. Yet God has promised children to Abram, so many they will number the stars, form and lead nations. So here, we have a little plot hole.

This type of narrative appears throughout the Old Testament—a fruitful womb, justification for the rape of the majority of the named women in the multitude of its pages. Sarai "gives" Hagar to Abram "in her place." As a result of this event, both violation and supplication, Hagar conceives.

Here, the translations of the text vary. Some say that as soon as Hagar realizes she is pregnant, she starts to "despise" her mistress; some use the phrase "look on with contempt." Regardless, something changes in Hagar, and Sarai does not take kindly to it. She complains to Abram that she is suffering at the hands of her servant; will he do something? Abram, central to the action yet insufferably passive, tells Sarai to do whatever she wants with Hagar. The vagueness here is telling. The translations all say Sarai "mistreats" Hagar, some even say "harshly." So Hagar flees, runs to the desert. She gets lost in the wilderness. What happens from there is interesting.

> "Now the angel of the LORD found Hagar by a spring of
>   water in the desert—
> the spring along the road to Shur. 'Hagar, servant of Sarai,'
>   He said,
> 'where have you come from, and where are you going?'"
> —Genesis 16: 7–8

~

ii.

We could start this story at the beginning. On a bridge, with a woman driving herself to a scheduled C-section. Planned, due to the fact of her unborn daughter's reluctance to enter the world in an orderly fashion. The baby is breech, positioned butt-first in the birth canal. That woman, in that car, has decided to name her backward daughter after her grandmothers: Jackie Kathleen or Kathleen Jackie. The baby's father, the woman's ex-husband of almost exactly nine months, is in the passenger seat. He turns to her.

Here, we have to fill in the details. We can imagine the skip of the tires over the rivets in the road. Maybe a pelican tucks its rusty wing into its neck on one of the pillars in the bay. He speaks. While he wasn't a fan at first, he says he's come around to the name. The man thinks it's a good one, both of their mothers together. The woman seethes in silence. After the doctors cut her open a few hours later and pull the baby from her womb, they ask her its name.

"I still don't really know what came over me," my mother tells me, many years later. "I just knew right then that I didn't want him to have anything to do with naming you. I just said, 'Rachel. Her name is Rachel.'"

I try not to attach too much symbolism to the details of my birth. I know most of them are coincidental. People get pregnant and have babies every day. But when I first learned about the concept of "nominative determinism," I went down a hole for hours. Simply put, this theory posits that people are drawn to careers or lines of work related to their surnames—a researcher named Richard Trench writing a book about subterranean London or a woman named Sally Ride who goes on to become an astronaut. Others have stretched this idea to more existential areas of focus, implying that our names' meanings, or the circumstances under which we were given them, may have some unconscious gravitational pull. I like this idea, even if it is a little woo-woo. I wonder if my mother naming me out of spite was a cosmic push. Without knowing it, she may have been trying to free herself (and by extension, me) of an ambivalent, if dutiful, man.

And yet—I was given my father's last name. Not hers. Until she remarried ten years later and I was legally adopted by her second husband, I still bore a part of my real father's identity. I often wonder why she was so stubborn about my first name but not my last. Maybe she knew things would change, that she had a new future waiting for her after this hurdle was cleared. Maybe my last name was always a placeholder. Even now, I keep my stepfather's last name. I did not change it when I was married. I joke that it was for convenience; my last name is four letters, my husband's thirteen. Mine looks better on a book spine. It does not connote any religious or ethnic distinctions. But that's not really why, not totally. I think I just wanted to stay who I was, even though a major part of my identity was changing, that I was yoking myself to another, a man who could potentially do the same thing my father had done to my mother. I did not believe he would—but better not to risk it.

Another coincidence of birth: my mother and I are both born under the sign of Aries, the child of the zodiac. Aries are known for their creativity, passion, and ambition; they are also known for their stubbornness.

iii.

I was a know-it-all child, and I learned to read at an early age. The stories came first from a children's picture-book Bible. Then, I worked up to *Teen Study Bible for Girls;* then the *Life Application Study Bible,* geared toward adults; then I asked my mom for *The Living Word* for Christmas, a little beat poetry. I liked the Old Testament the most, with all of the theatrics and burning bushes. Only the book of Revelation matched the Old Testament's drama, but those passages scared me a little bit, with their scrolls and horsemen.

I especially liked the stories about women. Like Jael, who drove a tent stake through the head of a sleeping would-be invader in order to save her people. Lot's wife, reluctant and headstrong, turned into sentient salt as punishment for feeling homesick. I looked up the story of Rachel, my namesake, with excitement, but was quickly disappointed. Her story was interesting to me, only in that she was described as being beautiful, while her sister had bad eyesight. I used those verses to torment my older sister Nickie, who was shy and wore thick Coke-bottle glasses.

I learned about my "mission field," my duty to "go out and make disciples of all men." In a youth group, during a tent revival, I got saved. Then, the work began—go out and preach the gospel to all who will listen. I went to church camp in the summer, joined the hundreds of spectators when Billy Graham came to Tampa on a stadium tour.

As I got older, the church lessons started to change. So did my body. We were divided by gender in Bible study. The boys studied the story of David, using a book called *Facing Your Giants* as their devotional. Us girls were given the story of Ruth, with Jackie Kendall's *Lady in Waiting: Becoming God's Best While Waiting for Mr. Right.* I remembered the story of David and Bathsheba, the juicy parts, the bathtub on the roof, and how rich she sounded, and rolling my eyes at the rest of the story's war and soap-opera plot. I was extremely jealous of the boys.

During our summer reading *Lady in Waiting,* I learned that my highest duty as a Christian woman, the real lesson I'd apparently waited years to mature into receiving, was modesty. We were encouraged to dress in a way that would not make young men "stumble." The boys could not be trusted not to act on their urges. Nobody mentioned our urges, and I wondered why. Maybe I was the only one who had them. But I doubted it. Regardless, I was capable of existing in the world alongside boys without foaming at the mouth or renouncing my faith on the spot if they showed too much ankle. I did not buy this double bind.

"You have to understand; they're just wired that way, Rachel," my mom said.

We were driving back across the bridge from church, and I was complaining about not being able to wear a two-piece bathing suit to the church pool party. I was twelve, and I thought the boys were getting off pretty easy. They splashed in the pool bare-chested, puka shell necklaces glistening, while the oversized black T-shirt I was required to wear over my bikini billowed in the water and stuck to my back in the Florida sun. I couldn't dive or do cheerleading moves in the water with all that extra fabric. It felt cruel that God would change my body, giving me the buds of breasts and a butt that sprang out fully formed, seemingly overnight, if they were burdens of sin to bear, to hide, to shield others from. I grumbled.

My mom cleared her throat. Without taking her eyes off the road, she said, "And just so you know, all the women in our family are very fertile. We can practically sneeze and get pregnant."

Those two sentences would be the only sex talk I'd ever receive.

Once I'd seen what was expected of me, church started to bore me. Boredom calcified into anger. The half-hour drives over the bridge made me restless, a black mood descending on me the closer we got to church. I started faking sick or claiming I had homework. As soon as my parents left for service, I'd open the computer cabinet in the living room and log on to LiveJournal and gURL.com, where I'd complain to online strangers about how strict my parents were. Those strangers, mostly other teenage girls, sent me their badly coded websites with archives of poetry and Fiona Apple lyrics. I'd spend hours online, shutting down the computer in a panic as soon as I heard the mechanical clack of the garage door opening, which meant my parents were home.

At school, I befriended the wildest girls in my grade, girls who shoplifted thongs from Charlotte Russe and positioned the straps just above their white, pocketless jeans. My friend, Madi, let me pierce her belly button with an ice cube and a sewing needle. I learned a lot from Madi, like how to roll the band of my Soffe cheerleading shorts perfectly so they showed two tanned half-moons of butt cheek, which had a cartoonish effect on the boys our age. I felt punch-drunk with the new realization that my body might not be a burden, but something more like a weapon—Jael's glittering stake to wield at my will. I started to notice men, godly or otherwise, scanning, lingering. Their gazes made me simultaneously giddy and terrified.

For a while, my mom held the reins as tightly as she could. I didn't have the courage to tell her I didn't believe in God. But she wasn't stupid, and we reached a sort of détente wherein I agreed to go to Sunday-morning Big Church and the occasional social event, but not to youth group. Something in me had shifted permanently when the heavenly gaze had turned so glaringly to my body. Once the crack was there, everything around me seemed aligned to widen it.

I finally listened to secular radio whenever I wanted, not just in surreptitious spurts on the lowest volume on the stereo after my parents went to bed. I made a to-do list of sins, things to cross off now that I wasn't a Christian. *Drink, smoke, shoplift.* I wanted to know everything, see how it felt not to be bound to ancient laws. I felt like Margaret Mead, if she took her notes in gel pen and wore body glitter.

The last item on the list I accomplished with a similarly anthropological determination. *Lose virginity.* I called the last boy I had dated, a nice-enough boy with a floppy emo haircut named Trevor. I went to his house after lunch period, while his parents were still at work, and informed him that we were going to have sex. We did so, and I left. The movie *Wimbledon* was playing. I never talked to him again. I was devastatingly underwhelmed.

All of that modesty, the paralyzing fear of fornication, and for what? Anyone who was a religious teenager knows that doing everything up to the point of actual intercourse is a gray area as far as "virginity" goes. I'd had my share of fun with my new friends, even before I fully cleaved myself from the church, and found that my zeal for making out was stronger than any holy spirit I'd caught in the pew. But I was crestfallen to discover that going all the way felt ... anticlimactic. Sex was so much more boring than fooling around in cars, show bathrooms, and at friends' houses. Doing hand stuff on a Honda's vinyl upholstery in the Florida humidity at least had some element of danger, be it a cop rapping on the window or a low-grade yeast infection. Of all the flavors of sin, losing my virginity ranked pretty low. Not worth the trouble.

~

iv.

> "Yet no deity comes to deliver her from bondage and oppression; nor does she beseech one. Instead, this tortured female claims her own exodus. Hagar does not cry out to any god, most especially to Yahweh."
> —Phyllis Trible, *Texts of Terror*

Maybe I should start with the day I bought a pack of balloons, streamers, candy, and toilet paper from Walgreens with my pregnancy test, in an embarrassingly obvious attempt to—what? Fool a cashier whose face I remember so clearly—her tattooed eyeliner, the papery tanned skin of her chest under her uniform vest—a woman who almost certainly has never thought twice about ringing up a pregnancy test on the side of US 19? Was I thinking the balloons would throw her off? Who knows? I still do this, sometimes, when I am buying embarrassing things—make an entire narrative out of impulse buys, try to make the cashier imagine a very different reality than the one I am in. The after part, though, that ought to have been the big movie moment, but I don't really remember it. I think it was in the grimy bathroom of my tiny apartment downtown, but it might have been somewhere else, maybe work.

Or we could start when I started to feel sick, I guess. I thought maybe it was just my job, week after week of climbing up and down two sets of stairs, ferrying baskets of fried shrimp and scallops to diners at Sloppy Pelican, the shitty beach bar and grill where I worked. My shifts were repetitive:

Clock in
Say hi to Pancho
Pick up tray
Load tray with baskets
Lift tray to right shoulder, balance with left hand
Descend stairs
Place baskets on tables
Stow tray between left arm and body
Ascend stairs
Take a deep breath before going back into the kitchen
Repeat.

After a while, the greasy air I inhaled started to feel like a physical weight in my lungs. Didn't help to smoke cigarettes with the barbacks behind the dumpsters. Didn't really hurt either. I felt like shit almost every day, a hungover Sisyphus rolling her sadness up the splintered stairs from the parking lot to the restaurant.

There was a red tide earlier that summer, and dead fish had washed up in droves, leaving a vague stench that came in on the occasional breeze, even months later. I slung frozen daiquiris for tourists and pitchers of beer to off-duty fishermen and the group of old men who showed up every morning at 10:30 on the dot. We called them the Breakfast Club. Most of them were vets. All were retired. They'd sit at the dock bar and shoot the shit until each of them had bought a pitcher for the group. I loved them. They kept my lights on. Thursdays were College Nights, where students from Eckerd College and Stetson Law came in droves for one-dollar beers and plastic test-tube shooters. I worked well past 3:00 a.m. on those nights, and after we'd wiped all the counters and put up the stools, my coworkers and I would head to Waffle House.

Almost nothing is as good as being at Waffle House after work, when the sun is coming up. Once, our favorite waitress had been arrested while taking our order, and we pooled our tips to help with her bail. This Thursday, though, the sight of my smothered and covered hash browns in the fluorescent light made me feel sweaty and prickly, and I excused myself to the bathroom and threw up my lunch. If I'm being honest with myself, I knew right away. *The women in our family.* A sneeze, remember?

In my twenties, I was more concerned with exploring the world through others than in the incidental bonus of forming romantic relationships. What could this person teach me about life, my body, writing, Colombia, the Bakersfield sound, *osso buco,* manual transmissions? After I dropped out, I moved back to my hometown, but not to my home. My family was disappointed in my lack of ambition, offended by my faithlessness and the error of my ways. All I cared about was working and saving enough money to get out of Florida for good. I had always wanted to leave, in some ways—to know what I might become if the variables of my life were shuffled like cards in a deck. I counted my tips, stashed them in a Crown Royal bag, stayed on my side of town, away from my parents, dreaming of skyscrapers.

Then, I met Justin.

A lot of that time is fuzzy, behind a haze of schwaggy weed and depression, but not the night I met him. It was hot, he wore a blue shirt with a torn pocket, and we left the bar to get cheeseburgers. He lived three blocks away from me. He was the first person I ever wanted so much I felt needy. Embarrassingly needy. It was not a familiar feeling. I was twenty-three. I loved him pretty much right away.

I'd never before had sex with someone I actually loved, or was falling in love with, and the difference short-circuited some part of my brain. I knew I couldn't let on, or whatever tenuous hold I had on him would fall apart. He'd been in a long relationship just recently;

he didn't want anything serious. We spent the end of summer riding around in his truck, swimming in the Gulf, together every night in sandy sheets, only to go our separate ways in the morning with little fanfare. But I strained at my yoke. I wanted something to cling to. One night, I told him, after several beers, how I felt. He politely declined to love me back, as I had known he would. I sank into myself.

On an early Tuesday morning, three weeks after my confession to Justin, two weeks after Waffle House, and a few days after Walgreens, I drove myself to Planned Parenthood. Tuesday, early, to avoid the crowds of protesters. I sat in the waiting room, reading my book about Greek mythology and wishing I was Daphne, shot through with a lead arrow. They called my name, and I headed through a doorway into a smaller room.

What I remember of the consultation comes in fragments, sensory details: cold gel, wishing I'd shaved my belly hairs. Florida law required that I sit through a "counseling session." I remember someone asking, "Has anyone coerced you into coming here today?" The sonogram tech, looking at the screen and not me, asking in a monotone voice if I wanted a printout, and then, "Would you like to be informed if there is more than one fetus?" A rushing of blood in my head, like a shell held up to your ear.

A medication guide being read out loud to me. My name being called out again. The rustle of paper as I took the first doctor-administered pill from a Dixie cup and the prescription for the next one. I walked back through the parking lot to my car. I don't remember being advised of any severe side effects, just that I should plan to take off work for the twenty-four hours following the second pill and to expect some light cramping.

I drove to Publix in a daze to gather supplies: soup, Gatorade, trashy magazines. What did I want to eat while administering my own at-home abortion? Interesting question. I stared at the rows of corn chowder and Italian wedding soup and three-bean chili. So here we are. Publix. This moment I remember with no confusion, not a single image blurred, perfect clarity. A familiar voice behind me.

"Knox!"

Jesus, I thought, then laughed at the thought of Jesus, probably orchestrating this moment in a last-ditch attempt at answering some red-faced protester's prayer.

I turned toward the voice. Justin stood at the end of the aisle, cradling a giant Zephyrhills water jug full of coins. He was, of course, smiling. He looked into my basket.

"What's up with all the soup? You sick?"

I looked at the jug instead of his face and thought about all the nights we'd stumbled into his moonlit room, his wallet and all of that loose change spilling out of his swim trunks when they hit the floor. He walked toward me. *Fuck.*

"Hey," I said, as cooly as I could manage. "Yea, under the weather. What are you up to?"

"Coinstar." He hoisted the jug. "Sorry you feel like shit. That sucks. Do you need anything?" He shifted his weight from one sneakered foot to the other.

I looked at him for a minute. He was trading in couch cushion treasure for cash to buy groceries. A few possibilities played themselves out in my mind, like a movie montage.

If I told him, he might drop everything to help me. He was a decent person. He'd get a new job, come to appointments, fall back in love with me as he realized it was fate. The old neediness and *wantwant-want* for him flashed violently in me, closed up my throat, subsided, made me queasy.

I couldn't weather another abandoning. The possibility that he might not do those things, that he would reject me again, call me a conniving bitch, accuse me of lying—highly unlikely, but even the idea of him hating me was one I could not bear to entertain.

I imagined a worse scenario: Even if he did the right thing, it wouldn't be because he loved me. It would be out of obligation, a sense of duty. In what universe could we ever be parents? He would feel, know, that his life was over, that he'd thrown away his future by involuntarily hitching himself to my busted wagon for the rest of his life. He would grow to resent me, drift away or push himself away from me, marry someone else, exchange pleasantries at pickup and drop-off. I imagined both of us, abjectly deferring our dreams in service of an as-yet-unreal third party, two bright futures blinking out into nothing.

You have to remember, I was just twenty-three. Maybe that seems old to you, old enough to know better, to make smarter choices. But it felt like my life was just beginning. This matters to me, even if it doesn't to you, that this moment felt so big I could not see around its corner.

So I made a choice.

"I'm good," I heard myself saying. "Just gonna go home and take it easy."

"Okay. Feel better, Rach. Good seeing you." A shrug and a smile.

I wandered the aisles until I saw that his truck had left the parking lot, then I went to the pharmacy counter to pick up my prescription. The pharmacist said nothing. I said, "Thank you." I got into my car and drove back to my apartment.

I took the first pill at the clinic, under the observation of the doctor, as prescribed by Florida law. I took the second one, the one I'd picked up at the pharmacy, a few hours later, according to the directions: dissolved under the tongue. I set the bottle of Tylenol with codeine on the counter warily, not sure why I'd been given such a strong painkiller. I hated downers, and anyway, they said it would basically feel like an unusually heavy period.

I'm not sure when I ended up on the bathroom floor, but the pain came on swift and horrific. One minute I was opening a can of soup, and the next I was crawling on the tile floor toward my tiny bathroom, racked with pain. My vision blurred and shook. I got as horizontal as I could.

From the angle I was lying, I could just barely see the TV playing the *I Love Lucy* box set I'd put on earlier. The pain was excruciating. I am not going to describe the nature of it because I can't. It knocked me out of the category of "one capable of describing" and into something else, something feral. I drifted in and out of focus. Lucy twirled around in a mink coat, Ethel told Lucy's fortune at the kitchen table, Lucy did ballet. I bled. And bled. And bled.

A little at first, and then a lot. I bled so much I thought I was dying. I may have been dying. Things got a little biblical. What the doctor hadn't told me, or I hadn't heard, or didn't remember, was that the first pill thins and softens the lining of the uterus. The second pill induces contractions. In very rare instances, lethal hemorrhaging can occur.

I passed out at least twice. The thought never occurred to me that something might be wrong, that this wasn't how this was supposed to go. It seemed just and deserved, the pain. God punishing me. My thoughts swirled around like snowdrifts, settling here and there. I thought about all of the images the protesters carried like signs on pieces of plywood—little photoshopped fingers and toes—then I saw Lucy and heard "vita-meata-vegamin" in a loop, like some kind of fucked-up Dante fever dream. I bled, and slept, and sweat, and cried, and bled.

I thought about attempting to reach for my cell phone, thought about calling my mom, remembered I couldn't, not about this. I tried, with difficulty, to focus on things that made me feel safe. My quilt, stitched from scraps by my grandma for my high school graduation. The part in "Free Fallin'" when the harmonies come in, the way Tom Petty breathes the words "Ven-tur-a Bou-le-vaaard." The familiar sounds of Tropicana Field, whistles and the crack of a bat and a pipe organ. Sucking the juice out of a boiled peanut, tossing the shell out of a car window. The sun in my apartment slanted through the blinds slowly, angled one way, then the other, then gone. I woke up in the middle of the night, when it had finally, miraculously cooled down, and pulled myself, crawling, to my bed. I was back working at the restaurant in two days.

I never told my mom, or anyone else. I'm telling it now, I guess, but I feel like I'm telling it all wrong. Which is maybe why I never tell it. Not shame, not really. Anxiety about delivery, about precision. What a wrong word might do. Afraid to fuck it up, you know?

~

V.

Sometimes, when I am alone, or sick and feverish, or I see a woman my age with a new baby, or when I am considering the trauma that my body has undergone, I remember the hours I spent on that floor. I was so desperately alone. All I wanted was my mom. She wasn't there, and that was another choice I made. Me, not her. When I told her a few months after that day that I was packing up to move, she told me how proud of me she was. She told me the story at the beginning of this one—her own. But telling it this time, she backtracked, starting somewhere new.

She and my father were signing the divorce papers and went out to a friendly-ish dinner. She had instigated the divorce because he was chronically unfaithful and had started selling drugs out of their apartment. They had some wine. She found out she was pregnant a few days later. (A sneeze.) She told me how she had thought, briefly, about making a choice not to have me. How she made an appointment and her best friend had driven with her there. How happy she was now, looking at me, that she changed her mind. How happy she was that I was going after my dreams, like she hadn't been able to, because she'd had babies to take care of. But it was all worth it because here you go and here you are. I wanted to tell her then, but she was so proud of me. It broke my heart in half.

This story makes me feel shame, anguish, rather than the joy or gratitude that I think she hoped to provoke. It makes me feel like a deserter. Like I abandoned my post. I realized when she told me that I couldn't, or wouldn't, probably, ever tell her what I'd done. Not now that I know what she did, having been in the same situation that I found myself in and made the noble, selfless, sinless choice. I cared about what my mom, not Jesus, would think of me, and I'd made the opposite choice. I thought if I kept the story to myself, I wouldn't risk fucking it up, and maybe she'd feel proud of me just a little while longer.

What kind of woman does that make me?

~

vi.

I learned from a professor, an expert in Hebrew linguistics, that the word "barren" in translations of the Bible is not fully accurate, at least not in the way it is commonly interpreted. To be barren, or *akara*, is not to be infertile. There is another version of that word, used interchangeably, with the slightest of spelling differences—*akura*. Its translation is "uprooted." In a sense: to be a tumbleweed, lost in the wilderness. The most informed translations make clear that to be childless in the Bible is a state of divine existence—not a medical condition, but a religious one. God, in his omnipotence, is the only decider of when a woman bears fruit. The land is not literally barren or *incapable* of being fertile; it just hasn't been planted yet. Nothing has taken root. Sarah, Rebecca, Rachel, and Leah all conceive on Rosh Hashanah. The text says they are *remembered* by God.

In her 2018 book *Motherhood,* author Sheila Heti wrestles with the decision to have a child. She consults friends, her partner who already has a child from a previous marriage, a psychic, and maybe most importantly, the I Ching. She uses a system of asking yes-or-no questions of the I Ching, then flipping a coin, each side corresponding to an answer. Over the course of the book, which is structured along the phases of a menstrual cycle, the reader witnesses Heti take up every side of this complicated decision—from wanting a baby desperately, imagining it and the kind of mother she would be, to solid determination that her art and this book itself supersedes the desire to become pregnant. At one point, she starts to consider a biblical story of Jacob grappling with an angel or demon or demon-angel (Heti seems as confused as I often am revisiting scripture), alongside her own struggles.

> "First he wrestles till daybreak. Then the creature touches the socket of Jacob's hip, and it is wrenched. Then the demon-angel asks to be let go, but Jacob refuses. Jacob says he will not let it go until the creature blesses him, so the creature does. Then Jacob names the place where he is standing, a single word that indicates: *Here is where I saw God face-to-face, and yet my life was spared.* Then he limps away with the sun rising at his back. All the fighting takes place at night . . . The most important thing is that Jacob continues to fight, even after he is injured, and instead of fear or anger toward the demon-angel, he asks to be blessed. I think that is the most moving part. That opens something inside me."

It opens something in me too; it gives me the permission to take my decision as seriously as one of biblical angel-wrangling. Much of my hesitation comes from knowing that my story is not the one that people use as counter-arguments—the serious cases that are cause for exceptions, those women who have been victims of rape or incest, who are carrying the embryos of their domestic abusers. I was not a victim, in this instance, of anything but circumstance. Convincing myself that I still deserved a choice, a chance, was harder than I'd expected. It helped to hear other stories, other women who'd made this choice in every imaginable situation. Religious women, already moms of three or four children. High-powered executive women, dedicated to a career. Athletes. Astronauts. Accountants.

In some ways, yes, I made the choice instantly, but that doesn't mean I made it lightly. Opponents of bodily choice seem to misunderstand that nobody, not one person, *wants* an abortion. It is not something one aspires to. It is only ever the result of intense and painful deliberation, the impossible comparisons of a before and an unknowable after, hypothetical guessing, wailing and gnashing of teeth. Every woman I know who made the choice to terminate a pregnancy did so after wrestling, mightily, with their own demon-angels. Considering myself as one in a long lineage of women who struggle to find their way through an existential desert, without a higher power to serve as a compass, helps me make some sense of the senseless.

Of course, all narratives serve a purpose. The Bible, one narrative spun out into countless translations and interpretations, serves whatever purpose an institution or preacher or parent wants it to. Translation offers the possibility of creative license, but it also allows for the insertion of opinion, which in turn is read as fact. The practical use of liturgical teachings shapes minds, households, nations, and teenage girls.

There is another definition of *akara*. Some have argued it means, more precisely, "stronghold" or "citadel." A linguistic neighbor of *akara* is the word *iqqer*, "to hamstring or cripple." The etymology does not make things make more sense.

Toward the end of *Motherhood,* Heti starts to wonder if the act of writing the book about the decision to have a child is the embodiment of her procrastination—the decision itself. "Maybe that's why I'm writing it," she says, "to get myself to the other shore, childless and alone. This book is a prophylactic. This book is a boundary I'm erecting between myself and the reality of a child."

How could she have known that when she set out on this project? She couldn't have, of course, but in the process of deciding, the decision was made. This is a problem unique to women of childbearing age and capability—the longer you wait to make a choice, the more you consider it, the more the choice itself, your agency, slips away from you. So you do your best with what you have at the time it happens. Considering a future in which I was an artist saved me, brought about my choice, in many ways.

"This book is a life raft to get me there," Heti writes. "For myself, that's all it needs to be—not a great ocean liner, just a barge. It can completely fall to pieces once I land on the other shore."

What you are reading is in many ways a patched, duct-taped life raft of my own—not the first one, which brought me to some essential shore, but the fourth, fifth, sixth rescue mission. In writing about my decision, I am making an attempt to justify my choices. I am saying, "Look, here, witness this. I didn't know where to start, where I had come from, or where I was going, but I made something, after all."

⁓

vii.

There have been many false starts to my story. People ask me all the time—now, years after the events I've just recalled—when I am going to have a baby. Like this story, my answer changes slightly each time I'm asked. A different version of events, depending on the narrative purpose I am looking to fulfill. I say, sometimes, that I don't know if I want to have children. This is not true. I say, other times, "We're not in a rush." This is a true statement, but it sidesteps the admission that there is no rush because there is no destination marked "baby" at all. Most often, I use humor to deflect. I joke that I *am* working on a baby; it's called A Master's Degree, it's called A Book, it's called A Career.

The real answers are myriad, and much more confusing. I save them for myself, when I am laying in the dark and let myself cycle through the questions: *Why did you do that? Why don't you want what so many people want?*

What's wrong with you?

Answers: I am normal. I am a monster. I have never wanted a child, I think, with certainty. Well, I backtrack—not really. Also: I feel like I do not deserve motherhood when I squandered it, when I fled to the wilderness of a life without. Also: I do not value motherhood, actually, as a personal achievement, and probably never will. And: I don't think having a child makes you a good person. I can think that people who have children are selfless and brave and also know that I am neither. That's not a bad thing, but it is true. Counterpoint: I'm really good with kids, good at taking care of them because I helped raise my brothers. Counter-counterpoint: That wasn't my decision, so it's different. I'm a better sister than I would be a mother. And: I feel like I threw away my chance at becoming a mother because it came at an inconvenient time. I feel like an evil person for feeling that the time was inconvenient. But: I feel like I did the right thing, the humane thing, by recognizing how ill-prepared I was. I was selfless, actually. I was looking out for myself, and isn't that what strong women do? Am I strong? I don't care. I care so much it aches.

I eventually met and fell in love with my now-husband, and this complicates things further. Part of me thinks I would have one with him if he wanted, and maybe that fact and all of my love for him would be an act of reverse-engineering myself into wanting and loving a child. He also does not want a child, and while this should make things easier, I am constantly frustrated by the fact that he does not have to answer any of these questions. I look at him when people ask it of me, and I seethe. I know that he knows how painful this question is for me, that he would gladly answer it in my stead, but loves me so much and so well that he knows it is immensely important to me to answer it by myself. This does not make me less angry.

He barely even needs to think about the question, really. Having a child would be something that happens *to* him, not something he makes happen—not fully. I feel mad about that, and then guilty, because I love him, and that isn't fair. Then, I feel sad and embarrassed. All of these emotions exist in me simultaneously, overlapping, cacophonous. I want to shout them at everyone who asks, my real answers, so they know, are forced to hear the shit I won't say to them: that I don't deserve a baby, that I don't want a baby, that I desperately want a baby, miss my baby, don't think of it as a baby, except sometimes when I do. That I think of myself as a baby, still, just like I was that day, cold and alone on my floor, in serious need of mothering, but kept from being mothered by my own choices. That I never gave my mother the choice because, by making her own difficult choice, she had given me one in the first place. The question kicks up a tangle of thistles and weeds, sends them rolling across the dusty landscape of my heart and my gut.

Sometimes I can't help feeling a guilt so profound it has a physical effect on me, racking my body with waves of nausea. I can't help it. I don't always want to. I sometimes listen to gospel music, when I feel homesick, especially. When a flight is turbulent, I backslide into panicked, silent prayer. I take walks on Sundays through my neighborhood past churches with the doors thrown open, with stained glass and mustard-colored pews, and ache at a loss that was completely voluntary. I stop and listen to the sermon for a minute and then I start walking again before I get stuck.

I wonder, often, about these biblical women.

For a while, I tried to look for solace in the story of my nominal counterpart, the story of Rachel. I was interested in the idea of God locking and unlocking wombs at His leisure. How much Rachel really wanted motherhood, or whether she wanted so badly to see her dream of being Jacob's wife realized that she would placate, deceive, and resort to the promise of aphrodisiac in mandrake roots. I never wanted to be that woman, and I had found myself so tempted. But the parallels weren't there, the story didn't bring me any relief or understanding. I stopped thinking about Rachel.

Ultimately, I had made my decision out of the desire I'd had my whole life, and one I wanted as much for myself as for any child I may or may not have: to be loved unconditionally, full stop—untethered to faith or a mother or guilt or adherence to rules and doctrine and the burden or blessing of a girl body. I wanted to be loved for the sheer fact of my lovability. When I couldn't find that in all the places it had been promised to me, I fled. It took years of wandering and solitude and bottomless loneliness, absolving myself, absolving my mother. All the old stories played a part—lamentation, repentance, forgiveness. My namesake wasn't the one to get me there, but Hagar was. We are not alike, not really, and anyway she is a character in a story. But there's a lot of power in the telling of a story, and in the reading of one—a messenger coming to you in the desert, pregnant and maybe dying. All by yourself, in exile.

Another wilderness will surely come along, and I'll write my way through that one too. But the fact that I can do that is a result of my choice, whether that choice was made for reasons anyone but me understands. It doesn't matter how many pages I write, how many questions I find answers to, how many times I repeat myself. It doesn't really matter how I tell the story, I think, as long as I do. That's what it was all for. For a future of telling stories. For other women to read them, to feel like theirs are valuable too, every single draft. Engraving them on little tablets of my own, offering them to you now, as proof that I kept my promise.

When I start to feel uprooted, when the deepest parts of me feel deserted, I say to myself, like a little prayer, "From where have you come, and where are you going?"

motel art

It was Easter in the South, and my mother was taking pictures of me and my sister Nickie in our Sunday best. We stood on the porch of the house on Church Street, itching at our white tights in the Florida humidity, clutching our wicker baskets full of plastic grass. We wore matching patent-leather Mary Janes. Nickie's were a few sizes bigger than mine and had no scuffs. We looked like a *Highlights* illustration, a dos and don'ts guide—her tall and brunette, not a hair out of place; me shorter and blonde and already, somehow, always sticky. Earlier that morning, my mother had struggled to smooth my hair into a ponytail and clip in a homemade barrette that she'd hot-glued fake pearls onto, snapping it against my skull with a thunk and a sigh.

In Sunday school, the teacher gave us all more candy for our baskets. I was last to reach into the bag, and all that was left were Airheads. I didn't really like Airheads, but candy was candy, and all of my teeth were sweet teeth. I took down two of the "White Mystery" flavor before Jesus had made it out of Gethsemane, followed by a strip of strawberry. Nickie grabbed my wrist to stop me from eating more and shot me a withering glare. I glared right back and popped another one, grape this time, into my mouth. She swiped the basket from me while managing to look straight ahead at the Sunday school teacher and put it just out of my reach. I pouted and fiddled with my dumb, frilly dress.

"It is finished," our teacher read. "The stone is rolled away. He is Risen."

Big whoop, I thought.

In Big Church, my stomach started to rumble. My mom was sitting next to me, all Aqua Net and adult braces, paying rapt attention to the announcements. Pancake breakfast next Saturday morning, clothing drive after the softball game that Thursday. My stomach gurgled, louder this time, and I squirmed. I couldn't do another fifteen minutes, let alone the usual two hours of this. I tugged on the sleeve of my mom's blouse and whined.

"Hush," she whispered.

"I don't feel good."

My sister shook her head at me. "She ate too much candy." They passed a look of commiseration between themselves. I stuck my leg out to kick my sister, hard, but she was too far away. My mom's eyes shifted to me and narrowed into alligator slits. There it was. I was gonna be in trouble. My stomach pitched and rolled.

"I need to go to the bathroom." We were almost at the praise chorus, and I was running out of time to get out of the sanctuary without causing a scene.

"Go. Quietly," my mom hissed. "And pull your dress out of the top of your tights this time." She angled to one side, knees pressed together, so I could squeeze by.

I walked down the aisle as fast as I could without making a racket. Once I was out of the sanctuary, everything stilled to a hush. My Mary Janes squeaked on the laminate flooring. I crossed the narthex into the church's "courtyard," a sad plot of dirt and weeds with crumbling sidewalk surrounding it on four sides. I traipsed through it in a panic.

Mosquitoes congregated around my sweaty forehead. Finally, I made it to the ladies' room.

I got through the Formica stall door just in time to hurl my ill-gotten gains into the bowl. I barfed for a while. Afterward, I rested my forehead against the porcelain, one arm slung around the base of the toilet. I got more horizontal. I didn't want to go back to church—to my mom, to the communion plate and the embarrassing and sancti-monious altar call, old ladies weeping into their walkers.

In the bathroom, I laid on my stomach, one chubby cheek on the cool tile. I could see underneath the door and the length of the wall across from the bathroom stalls. A huge painting took up most of the length of that wall. It had been there as long as I could remember.

It was not a painting, though, not actually. It was printed on can-vas, but it wasn't the real thing; it was a reproduction of Thomas Kinkade's *Bridge of Faith*. In the frame sat a sun-dappled cobblestone bridge, spanning two lush landscapes. A brook ran underneath it. The wildflowers along the banks were rendered in fuchsia, coral, and lav-ender. The colors reminded me of the unicorns on my sister's Trapper Keeper; of my stepmom's acrylic nails, a Marlboro 305 dangling in her bony hand. I fought the urge to throw up again. I pulled myself up from the floor and looked into the bowl of the toilet as I flushed.

Years ago, I was back in undergrad, enrolled in a nonfiction writing class at a liberal arts college in New York City. The class met in a room on Fifth Avenue and Fourteenth Street at the University Center: a giant glass-and-steel architectural art piece slammed down south of Union Square Park like an errant asteroid. Everyone was a fashion student, or a painter, or an activist, and they were all a decade younger than me. The assignment asked us to brainstorm an idea for a piece of cultural criticism. My classmates shared their plans for works of experimental, hybrid prose exploring works of art I'd never heard of, hyperspecific Tumblr aesthetics, and schools of Soviet philosophical theory that sounded like New Wave bands. I had no idea what any of them were talking about.

I thought about the art I was familiar with, having heretofore considered myself an extremely artistic and cultured person, and felt a flush of embarrassment. Who was I to be crafting cultural criticism when I barely understood the concept? My arts education consisted mostly of the musty *Time Life* picture books about art history that my grandma had used in her elementary school classroom—Degas's ballerinas, the requisite Renaissance classics, Picasso, Van Gogh, and your occasional Rothko, if the publishers were feeling modern in 1967. Outside of those pictures, though, I didn't generally interact with art in my everyday life. Except, of course, for kitsch. I saw that kind of art everywhere. Wall hangings, embroidered throw pillows, trivets and mugs and calendars and glossy, pearlescent Christmas ornaments, all bedecked with cottages and wildflowers and endless, golden light. I saw Kinkade everywhere.

I have trouble articulating the art I'm an expert in, because most people wouldn't consider it art. The aesthetics of the form I know deep in my bones appeal to a very specific slice of the population: the white, lower-class, Evangelical Christians of the southeastern United States. I could give a TED Talk on the denomination-specific iconography of the crosses tattooed on the sunburnt backs of bikers. In Missouri, there's a Precious Moments Museum; I could be a docent, given my experience as the granddaughter of a collector whose display case for the porcelain angels was the epicenter of her home. I wish they offered PhDs in Joanna Gaines so I could write a dissertation on how her Magnolia empire has steered a whole new generation of God-fearing young women toward shiplap and sandalwood.

And that's just the newest wave. Before them was the earlier generation: the old-school, tent-revival Billy Graham-ericana that decked
out so many double-wides and nursing homes from the Blue Ridge
eastward with "Footprints in the Sand" plaques and Promise Keepers
bumper stickers that now fill the shelves of my local Goodwill.

I feel queasy about Kinkade because, by lining the halls of Southern
churches and the homes of people who love the religion that troubles
me, he's come to be my own boogeyman. He's inseparable from some
of the parts of my past that I don't like remembering. Kinkade reminds
me of that church bathroom, that church, those people. For those
reasons alone, I should probably be among the chorus of his critics,
but something in me is resistant to that route. I loved some of those
people, loved to be in a room of covered dishes and open laps. But
there are other parts of those memories that I won't let myself forget,
that won't be pushed out by the warm glow of the others.

So much of art is made up of what the viewer brings to it, whatever
existential baggage they've schlepped with them to the art gallery, the
movie theater, the pages of a novel. Once an association is made, it's
hard to shake. Many of the memories of my childhood in Florida are
garish and candy-colored, like Kinkade's cottages—dreamy and extrav-
agant and sometimes unsettling. Kinkade's work often decorated the
set pieces of those memories, like the *Bridge of Faith* in that bathroom
or the wall calendar at the home of the family who babysat us when my
mom was working. I think about Kinkade a lot when I think about that
time. Sometimes he makes me nostalgic, but often, he makes me sick.

I enjoy a bunch of things that make me sick, though. All of us do.
That doesn't make them inherently worthy of dismissal or ridicule. I
grew up in Florida, home of Mickey Mouse and Margaritaville. My
city is the birthplace of Hooters, whose slogan for most of my life
was "delightfully tacky, yet unrefined." I want that on my tombstone.

Kitsch makes me happy; it's where I feel most at home. *Vanderpump Rules* was nominated for two Emmys last year. Taco Bell has an entire lit mag dedicated to its lowbrow genius.

Most of the people who are obsessed with Kinkade have their feet planted firmly on the side of either adoration or hatred for the painter. Everything written about him is sneering or saint-making; there's no in-between. Their minds are made up. Mine is not.

I went down the rabbit hole that was Thomas Kinkade's life, his life's work. I stayed up all night reading every reference linked on his Wikipedia page. I watched YouTube videos ripped from old TV interviews and Christmas specials. I read a horribly written biography, *Billion Dollar Painter,* while researching Kinkade's past. It was written by G. Eric Kuskey, an old colleague of Kinkade's, and it read more like a hagiography than a recounting of real events. Kuskey thought the guy was a marketing genius, but thought little of the art itself.

I found a podcast episode about Kinkade, hosted by an art critic and an art historian, titled "Should Thomas Kinkade Paint Trump's National Portrait?" He couldn't, of course, because he's dead. He overdosed six days before my birthday years ago.

I kept finding out things, some that made me laugh, some that impressed me, some that drove me crazy. In an increasingly "pick-a-take" culture, I just couldn't find a place to land when it came to him. What was it, truly, about this artistically average, obscenely wealthy, hypocritical, dead-in-his-bed Californian con man that kept needling at me?

Thomas Kinkade—self-described "Painter of Light"—was an American painter who specialized in idyllic scenes of snow-dusted cabins, pastorals, and rays of sunshine beaming over meadows. His work was almost universally panned by critics as kitsch, but found a receptive audience in the Evangelical Christian congregation throughout much of the nineties. Kinkade sometimes incorporated religious themes into his work—church houses, crosses on a hillside, the Nativity scene covered in a peaceful layer of snow (a true artistic liberty, as temperatures generally hover in the high fifties in Bethlehem in December).

Here's the basic gist. Thomas Kinkade grew up poor in California, the son of a single mom. He went to UC Berkeley and then a fancy art school in Pasadena. He got a job as an animator and painter for movie sets, where he became fascinated with light. He started making small paintings of landscapes and cottages, selling them at art fairs around California. He almost never painted people; his landscapes are unfailingly empty, although they often give off the appearance of someone having just left, the painting capturing the stillness of nature and domesticity when we cannot see it. He began to insert Christian themes and symbols into his art—crosses and chapels and countryside churches—and people loved these paintings. His success grew, and he founded his own studio. From there, he started mass-producing his work to keep up with demand, mostly from religious customers. He'd make a painting, mass-produce prints of that painting, and then employ a team of protégés and students to embellish these prints with hand-painted accents—light and shadow and leaves—assembly-line style.

In her book about California, *Where I Was From,* Joan Didion describes Placerville, the town where Kinkade grew up, and about his painting of a Mohawk territory landscape that adorns the Yosemite National Park visitor center, entitled *The Mountains Declare His Glory.* Didion quickly outlines Kinkade's trajectory as an artist in her spare, smart style, and then starts to describe his art in a way that knocks me out:

"A Kinkade painting was typically rendered in slightly surreal pastels. It typically featured a cottage or a house of such insistent coziness as to seem actually sinister, suggestive of a trap designed to attract Hansel and Gretel. Every window was lit, to lurid effect, as if the interior of the structure might be on fire."

These paintings sold en masse, leading to the existence of Thomas Kinkade gallery stores, which popped up in malls across the country, franchised to private owners (most of them Evangelical entrepreneurs, spurred by the thought of supporting a fellow Christian businessman). The prints were licensed, as would be thousands of other Kinkade products—truly, too many iterations to name here, bordering on the absurd. According to his estate, at one point in the early 2000s, a Kinkade print or painting hung in one in every twenty homes in America. Thomas Kinkade's body of work, in my mind, has always been the peak of this brand of mainstream Evangelical art, the closest white trash has ever come to the hallowed halls of The Art World™. I don't know how to feel about the fact that they wouldn't let him in.

Kinkade himself was raised in the Church of the Nazarene, a Protestant sect characterized by their focus on missionary work in other countries and Wesleyan methodology. Kinkade died of an overdose of alcohol and diazepam in 2012, although you will not see this fact on many Christian websites eulogizing the painter; "natural causes" is the phrasing of choice.

When trying to write about Kinkade for the assignment on cultural criticism, I didn't really know how to talk about art on an academic or theoretical level. I'm still not sure if I do. I've never been capable of standing in front of a sculpture at a museum and articulating to my companion that it's actually a neoliberal excoriation of factory farming, or whatever. But I do like to look at art, as do most sane humans of all backgrounds. I love to walk around a gallery slowly, in a cool outfit, preferably with someone I want to sleep with; to arrange my face to look both contemplative and serious. I like being both contemplative and serious. I like craning my neck to read the placards under each work, letting them tell me how I should feel. I'm a big fan of a guided tour. When I talk to people who "get" art, though, I find myself envious. I wish I had their language, their eye, their understanding of all of the different schools and their histories. There is a currency to the sophistication of their minds, their expertise.

~

Is it really so bad to tell the stories that people want to hear? In *Billion Dollar Painter,* Kuskey writes that "Thom's consumers were so ravenous and faithful, it was like making money by accident."

After moving to New York in my twenties, hoping to start my life as an artist by going back to school, I realized that the place where I was raised seemed amusing to a lot of people. Every time I was introduced to someone or found myself explaining the pieces I was writing in my classes, it came up. "Rachel's from Florida, but we don't hold that against her." I didn't know how to feel about the jokes. True, it wasn't like I'd been raised in some major art city, like my classmates from New York or LA. I didn't have their sort of "academic" parents, but we weren't exactly hillbillies either. But sometimes, it was just easier to let people think we were.

I'd always thought I had it pretty good, considering my parents were both employed and educated. When I'd get into specifics of my upbringing, though, it felt like we came from different worlds. The colloquialisms of my Southern grandma sent them into fits of giggles, and they marveled at the boiled peanuts I made for our workshop party, turning them around in their hands like artifacts of an ancient civilization. An essay I wrote about manatees revealed that over half of my classmates were not aware they were actual, non-mythical creatures. I was shocked. Sometimes the reactions were irresistible, and I leaned into the jokes—exaggerated, embellished. It was just too much fun. Plus, they seemed to like that me better, maybe because I was not that me anymore; I presented like an ex-Floridian, far away from that life, reformed into a New Yorker. I could laugh about Florida Rachel, my own narrative creation, and make fun of her from some kind of distance.

I still write about these parts of my life over and over again because people seem to want to read it. About the swamps and the drugs and the trailer parks and the guns. They are all real, but I wonder how much I am misremembering. I wonder how much I am bending to an audience. "I was hoping you were going to say more about the uncle in prison. Could you expand there?" When I write about Florida, the feedback is always correlative, comparative, a connection must be made to the recent uptick in Florida stories: Have you read Carl Hiaasen? Have you seen *The Florida Project*? Did you watch that episode of *Atlanta*? Did you see that news story where the guy traded a baby alligator for a six pack? Did you see what the governor said about blah, blah, blah?

I don't feel insulted or overlooked by those comparisons, just kind of disappointed. It's hard to tell what others have exaggerated and what I've internalized. The case with Florida, usually, is a mixture of both. Sometimes I set out to tell one story and remember another one, one I would never tell because I am just now realizing its weight, how deeply I buried it in my attempt to not be a person-from-there and just a person.

~

Some of the arguments against Kinkade feel arbitrary to me, even if I want them to be true for my dislike to be justified theoretically. If one claims that his art is valueless because of its mass production, its scale, how are we supposed to feel about Andy Warhol? If we say that Kinkade was a bad man who abused women, and that this fact should negate his art's merit, what about Carl Andre, Picasso, Edward Hopper—just to name a few of the legion of bad art men? You could, I think, argue that Kinkade's benefactors and business partners exploited his growing reputation to further their own capitalist interests, knowing that middle- and lower-class Americans found it appealing that someone "just like them" was representing their values and surroundings. You could see, from our current political climate, how an imaginary, sun-dappled countryside of the past could be turned into a profitable and endlessly reproducible package, one used to sell people on a promise of a Pleasantville-style future (for a select few) that will presumably never be possible. This is a good reason to criticize Kinkade, but he's not even close to the only artist being co-opted by politicians (ask Tom Petty or Bruce Springsteen how they feel about it). That's a way bigger can of worms, how art imitates life, and life commodifies art.

But if it's that Kinkade's subject matter—natural landscapes and sites of faith and contemplation—are not high-concept enough to be called art, there I have a bone to pick. Tell it to Monet's garden bridges, Vermeer's domestic interiors, Seurat's merry riverbank sitters. This argument is the one that falls apart the quickest to me because I think, *Tell that to The Highwaymen.*

I wish I could remember the first time I saw a Highwaymen painting, but I can't. My guess is that you can't either, but I'm almost positive, if you happen to have grown up in or currently live in Florida, that you have seen one. Maybe not a true original Highwaymen painting, done by one of the two dozen or so founding members of the painting collective known by that nickname who operated up and down A1A and I-95 in the mid-century, but probably one of their protégé's work or an imitation of one. They decorate the halls of the state museums now, fetching many thousands of dollars in the resale market after their induction into the Florida Artists Hall of Fame in 2004. But before the rediscovery and recognition of their impact, most of the High-waymen's paintings decorated homes, offices, and small businesses throughout Florida. The descendant of one of the Highwaymen, Kelvin Hair, described the work of his father and his contemporaries as "motel art." It's true that these are the kind of paintings that exist pleasantly in the background of a space you're visiting—they usually feature things like palm trees, placid lakefronts, birds alighting on a pier—but they're so much more than that.

Alfred Hair was a fourteen-year-old high school student in Fort Pierce when his art teacher, Zanobia Jefferson, introduced him to Albert "Beanie" Backus, a local painter who had been formally trained at Parsons School of Design in New York City. It was 1956, and young Black men like Alfred had little access to the kind of arts education afforded to others. Backus encouraged Hair and another young Black artist, Harold Newton, among others, to focus their attention on painting. Newton, especially, was steered by Backus away from the mostly religious art he had been painting on velvet and selling to churchgoers toward landscapes and nature scenes. Harold would watch Beanie paint in his studio for a few hours, then return home and paint a similar scene, seemingly from memory.

While the young men didn't exactly receive formal training, they learned by observation, and they learned quickly. Gallery representa-tion was impossible in the Jim Crow South, so Newton started selling paintings out of the trunk of his car. One of fourteen children, Harold Newton had previously worked in the orange groves around Gifford and found that the money he could get for his paintings far outpaced what he made doing manual labor. Alfred Hair saw the money to be made and sped up the process they'd both learned, sometimes creating up to twenty paintings a day and famously selling them while the canvases were still wet. The two men shared what they'd learned with friends and others in the predominantly Black community of Fort Pierce, and gradually their numbers grew, along with a profitable new industry that allowed Black artists more than just economic leverage; it gave them the cultural capital to travel around Florida with slightly less fear of harassment than usual.

Alfred's method—painting as many works as possible, as quickly as possible—was adopted by many of the other artists in the collective. He told people that his goal was to be a millionaire by the time he was thirty-five. Newton, however, favored attention to artistry over quick production, and was known among the group as the most technically skilled. To this day, his works are the ones that fetch the most money, with a few exceptions from a notably exceptional artist herself: Mary Ann Carroll, the lone Highwaywoman.

When I started learning about the group, it was Mary Ann who captured my interest. Because she was a woman, yes, duh, but also because of the details of her life. Legend has it that Mary Ann, single mother of seven children, saw Harold's car, which was painted with bright flames. When she asked about them, Harold invited Carroll to learn how to paint, and she joined the group shortly after. Mary Ann was tough by all accounts; she was friendly with the men, but did not join them in their barroom off-hours. Instead, she returned to her children and spent much of her time involved in her local church. She was known to load up her car with as many paintings as she could fit, stating that she didn't have time to waste.

So why doesn't anyone know who The Highwaymen are? They're known more now than they were at the time they were working, for sure, but I was never taught about them in Florida public schools. There were no Highwaymen wall calendars for sale at the mall or at the visitors' centers along the state's highways. No mass-produced holiday ornaments, no collaboration with Disney World, unlike Kinkade. Interestingly, The Highwaymen's collective exchange of artistic skill is almost a mirror image of the way Kinkade's assistants worked. Where Kinkade's signature appeared on all of the prints, lithographs, and reproductions of his work, even though they were largely created by anonymous assistants, The Highwaymen were able to establish individual careers as artists due to Backus, Hair, and Newton's willingness to pass on their knowledge with no desire for ownership.

It's interesting, too, how so many of the artists came from religious backgrounds, like Harold Newton. Mary Ann Carroll, in her post-Highwaymen years, eventually became the founder and pastor of the Foundation Revival Center Church in Fort Pierce and was known for her devout faith. In his book about Carroll, Gary Monroe describes The Highwaymen's art as directly connected to spirituality. The distinguishing characteristics of a Highwaymen painting are in some ways reminiscent of the "God light" of Kinkade's work. In a Highwaymen painting, though, rather than the light seeming pale yellow, coming from above, the light is shockingly vibrant, in shades of deep red, navel orange, and the bright purple of jacaranda trees leaping off of the canvas—anything but pastel. Monroe describes the saturation of their colors and the sketchy, gestural shapes of the trees and creatures in the landscapes, saying that they "reinforced the idea that their art was divine, natural and wild—God with a tropical twist."

I am not one to judge whose faith is more sincere than anyone else's, or how an individual relationship to God did or didn't affect either Kinkade or The Highwaymen's visual styles. All I know is what I feel when I look at the paintings themselves. It's possible that I'm projecting all of this, that I'm seeing The Highwaymen's Florida with none of the baggage I bring to Kinkade's cottages and seasides. That I just *want* their art to be better. But if I'm the judge, it just is. Maybe an artist's connection to the divine is not so different from that famous saying about porn—you know it when you see it.

And I do see it—the connection to some kind of higher power—in the art of The Highwaymen. I've pored over the paintings in Monroe's book, in museums, and at antique markets. It's one of my life goals to own one of Mary Ann's paintings. Alas, since the Hall of Fame induction, the going rates for Highwaymen originals have skyrocketed. As of this writing, I am still, myself, a starving artist. But the paintings reflect something on canvas that I've never been able to articulate in words: the big, irrepressible power of Florida's topography, the way its islets and egrets and Everglades render me humbled and speechless. Where Kinkade feels like a charlatan, where he leaves me wanting, Highwaymen paintings strike some metaphorical harpsichord in my heart. They feel holy to me, in a way I can't explain.

~

Like Thomas Kinkade, artist Jeffrey Vallance went to art school in California when he was a young man. His family was upper-middle class and lived in Redondo Beach; Kinkade's mother was a single parent in rural Placerville. Vallance's "Infiltration Art" style earned him praise among the modern art crowd of the early eighties. Vallance's work is conceptual, political, concerned with pop culture and institutions. A notably un-cited section of his Wikipedia page describes his oeuvre as "tampering within bureaucratic structures to create change without creating conflict"—whatever that means. Vallance once posed as a janitor at a museum to replace existing electrical sockets with ones he'd painted himself, and at one point, he built an entire museum dedicated to Richard Nixon. For another project, he pretended to lose his wallet all over government buildings in Washington, DC, and created an exhibition of the letters he received when the wallets were mailed back to him. Vallance wrote a book imagining the life cycle of a chicken he bought at the grocery store, complete with a eulogy and funeral. The tastemakers of the time ate it up.

In 2004, Vallance proposed an idea for a new exhibition. He would curate a collection of Kinkade's work, both originals and the licensed objects and miscellanea sold across the country. Vallance's art-world cred lent some gravitas to the exhibit, one that the gallery imagined would be framed by irony. He aimed to make a statement on the capitalist nature of Kinkade's trademark sprawling production. In an essay about the exhibition's creation, Vallance writes:

"I took my job as curator very seriously . . . I wanted one example of everything mass-produced, which amounted to thousands of items, a real Noah's Ark-load of Kinkades. Samples of Kinkade's products had to be obtained from all of Kinkade's different manufacturers, including ceramics, lamps, fabrics, books, Bibles, videos, audio CDs, furniture, toys, miniature villages, mantel clocks, grandfather clocks, watches, blankets, figurines, snow globes, Christmas ornaments, Santa Claus figurines, Christian kitsch, greeting cards, dolls, teddy bears, quilts, calendars, nightlights, spice racks, umbrellas, coffee, model train sets, model cars and trucks, and promotional material on his log cabins and housing tracts. There was also a three-dimensional recreation of 'Bridge of Faith' (based on Kinkade's painting *The Bridge of Faith*), consisting of a life-size functional wooden bridge over an artificial babbling brook surrounded by attractive plastic flower arrangements."

The idea was greenlit and met with mixed reactions from the art world. Kinkade had agreed to the co-opting of his art and seemed thrilled to have a "real" gallery dedicated to his body of work. In a videotaped press conference about the exhibit, Kinkade was cheeky—seemingly "in on the joke"—smirking and fielding questions from journalists and art critics about the controversy with a dismissive air. He argued that the exhibition was a pushback against the elites of the art world:

"Art should be about embracing the culture in which the artist lives, and presenting something that forms a reaction, good or bad. A lot of artists are motivated, as you describe it, to walk the cutting edge, and they would believe that to urinate on a canvas, or take elephant dung and smear it on a religious icon, is a cutting edge that would demand attention and a reaction. Interestingly, I paint pretty pictures that are homespun, nonthreatening imagery, and the *London Times* calls me the most controversial artist in America. Just think how good I could do if I'd used elephant dung."

I might have agreed with Kinkade on some level, until I came across the photograph of the "Bridge of Faith" recreation. This bridge was so tied to my memory, to the wall of that bathroom at my church. To a building where I spent so many hours with all of the people I loved, people who devoted their lives to helping others and building a community. In this church, my mother, single with two young daughters, found a surrogate family. Women who babysat us while she worked, attended her wedding to my stepfather in dresses they bought on layaway, delivered casseroles to our house after she suffered a miscarriage. To see "Bridge of Faith," the image I'd looked at hundreds of times, now in the middle of a poured-concrete room, harshly lit, surrounded by gaudy fake flowers, with an intentionally sparse placard, presented as a punch line—it made me angry.

It evoked the same lava bubble in my stomach that I get when someone imitates a Southern accent, sticking out their top teeth and curling their lip back. Their "y'alls" are too pointed, none of the rolling molasses is there in the vowels where they should be. It's the same feeling I get when I see art-school kids wearing Carhartt WIP at readings in six-figure apartments, a weird fashion-y version of the clothes my uncles wear to work. I feel it when people mimic a banjo's strings, the tune of that song from *Deliverance,* to characterize a trip into a town that they deem threatening because of its distance from anything urban. I was not amused.

~

Kinkade's paintings, turned into prints and mugs and porcelain Christmas ornaments in Hallmark stores and Walmarts across every corner of America—if all of that art doesn't count as actual art, if it's something to scoff at—and it probably is—what, then, am I? If he'll never enter the halls of history because of the sheer popularity of his work and who it appeals to, what does that say about me? I want to make money from my art, but I also want people from where I am from to see it as real, as honest. Maybe not an exact copy of their particular lived experience, but recognizable in its shades and contours. I want them to see its truth and feel encouraged.

I don't think Jeffrey Vallance is some kind of genius, or even mostly correct about Kinkade. Both of them are from California, after all. But their exhibition gets under my skin in a way that feels . . . familial. I'd imagine that's the point, that someone swilling scotch in an etched crystal tumbler might argue that it's supposed to make you *think,* that it's not pure mockery under the guise of subversion. But that's just something people say when they're making fun of something. How could Kinkade, with all of his legendary business acumen and sensitivity for being perceived as an amateur, or an outsider, not see this for what it was?

What I think is more likely, and so much more frustrating, is that he saw it very clearly, indeed. He may have been so hungry for acceptance as to let it happen, regardless of how it made him look. He would finally have the milestone he craved: an exhibition in a modern gallery, and with it, the appearance of legitimacy. Any critique of his talent could be dismissed as elitism with a "Real Artist" behind him, even if Vallance was smirking while patting him on the back.

I relate to that double-edged hunger Kinkade may have felt, a desire for the blessing of a group of critics or readers who may not value the work of my peers or "the culture in which the artist lives"—which, here, would mean my part of Florida, right now. I wonder whether the only elements of my work that make it valuable are exploitative, if I can contain both my past and my present, and whether the responsibility to do so is even mine. Jokes about the South in general, and Florida in particular, are endless. Colorful. Sometimes I participate in crafting them. When people praise the work I make about where I am from, are they like Vallance—smirking while patting me on the back?

In *The Artist in the Mall,* Vallance describes that he designed the Kinkade show to work on three levels. The first audience was die-hard Kinkade fans: "For faithful Kinkade fans it was like a pilgrimage to the ultimate Kinkade Shrine. I observed Kinkade's collectors pointing out which objects they had in their collections, which pieces they would like to have, and which ones they were seeing for the first time. For them the show was truly heaven on earth." The second audience Vallance anticipated were members of the art world: "For the jaded contemporary art viewer it was over the top yet organized into what appeared to be contemporary art installations so that even if they hated Kinkade, they liked the show." Vallance also observed a third group, however, who saw it on both levels at once. For those viewers, the show presented a conundrum. "The only problem was when someone got trapped on the wrong level of perception. For example, if a contemporary-art person became trapped on the Kinkade-collector level and could not transcend the kitsch, it was excruciatingly painful for him or her. More rarely, if a Kinkade collector somehow got a glimmer that contemporary art was afoot, it unsettled him or her." In reflecting on the show's impact, Vallance noted that few opinions on Kinkade changed as a result of the show: "Most people entered and exited the exhibition at the same level as their belief system."

I wonder about my own belief system, how it affects my opinions of art. Specifically, I wonder if I am imbuing The Highwaymen's art with more significance simply because they are from Florida. Is that not reason enough, though? Why can't that be the sole foundation for my affection? When I look through the Florida Artists Hall of Fame, I see that there is not a single artist from St. Petersburg or Tampa on the list, which spans several decades. Why not? I can think of a dozen people who deserve to be on that list, that have made art I care deeply about, simply because it reflects the place that I love in some way. The problem is most of these people are outsiders—not in the way Vallance meant, as an ideological or artistic viewpoint. I mean they aren't part of the conversation. They are poets and painters and musicians and dancers, and the only thing that connects them is their fierce love of a place that does not seem to want them here.

Maybe, though, that is changing. At the 2025 Grammys, a glimmer of hope: rapper Doechii, Blake High School's finest, won Best Rap Album for *Alligator Bites Never Heal,* a mixtape shot through with Florida, inescapably a product of place. In her acceptance speech, Doechii gave her hometown its flowers: "I call myself the Swamp Princess 'cause I'm from Tampa, Flori-DA," she declared, telling labels to look there for new artists. "Go to Tampa, there's talent there, okay?"

I feel hopeful that there will always be Florida artists, even if the rest of the world doesn't always see them the way I do. I do not know if I have the talent to count myself among them, if I can transcend kitsch. Is there space in the public imagination for reconsideration of the South? In the art world? I hope so. I want a thousand Doechiis to grow up here and stay here to make their music. I want us to take home more Grammys, more Oscars, a National Book Award. I want more books and art and culture from all of the voices that make this place the wild, teeming landscape that it is. I want Highwaymen paintings to go for a million dollars (after I finally get one, obviously). I want thoughtful and nuanced art about Florida to be the rule, not the exception.

I write in the hopes that the truth of my experiences will do the opposite of Vallance's exhibition. Mine cannot be the only voice like it, saying, "Yes, that's what I am, but that is not all that I am." I want to hear all of those stories.

My mom and I had lunch recently, and she brought up a trip our family took to Europe. I hadn't thought about it in years. I was in my early years of college, and Nickie was teaching English at an international school in Prague. Over summer break, we visited her, stopping first in parts of Germany and Austria, where my mother had spent parts of her childhood as an Air Force brat. My three younger brothers were too little to understand the "foreign" culture of the cities we visited. In Vienna, they rolled their eyes when I said I wanted to go to the Belvedere, opting to go to a natural history museum that had dino-saur fossils instead. My mom came with me to the museum, patiently walking from room to room with me, until finally, we stood in front of *The Kiss,* Klimt's gilded masterpiece. I'd seen it, in replica, on the posters sold in my campus bookstore, and on the covers of journals in the Barnes & Noble at the mall. I couldn't believe I was standing in front of the real thing, in this huge museum on palatial grounds in Vienna, the city of Mozart and Beethoven. I bought a magnet that featured *The Kiss,* accented with gold leaf and lacquered in resin. Afterward, we rejoined the rest of the family.

We stuck out everywhere we went on that trip, my brothers all wearing bright orange-and-blue Florida Gators sweatshirts, my dad in cargo shorts and tube socks. I wore a droopy knit hat and dark jeans everywhere we went in Europe, trying to blend in by adopting a sort of boho-chic-on-layaway look. But it was a pointless endeavor, especially on the afternoon when my youngest brother, Jack, ate too many donuts at the hotel breakfast bar and, carsick on the van ride to an ossuary in the Czech Republic, threw up all over himself. Nickie gave him her sweatshirt to wear and shivered while he walked around in it all day, the too-long sleeves dragging into puddles of rainwater. We were an American mess.

"I remember you cringing across five countries. You were so embarrassed of us," my mom recalled, years later. I twinged with regret when I heard that. I thought most people looked back on their formative years with some reluctance. Everyone has a terrible haircut or a hacky sack phase they aren't proud of. But this was something deeper, and something I still chafe against all of the time.

I had wanted—still want, so badly—to be worldly. To be recognizable as someone who knows something about art or culture. A global citizen, not some dumb hick. Instead, I'd just displaced my own insecurity by putting it onto my family, whose only fault had been in being from where they were from. And I was from there too. And there we were—in *Europe!* And my mom had been there, had actually grown up there. She knew the names of all of the towns on the map and relished the food at the cafés we went to, and still spoke some German, *thank you very much.* We were privileged in so many ways: the means to travel, as a family of seven people, a not inconsequential cost; an eldest daughter with a master's degree, educating the children of diplomats and policymakers in a foreign country. My parents brought us to museums when we could afford it, read constantly, loved history and old movies and nature. So what was I so embarrassed of?

I think about that day in church, confronted with Kinkade and the complexities of self-perception his work provokes. I think about

the pages of that Sunday school Bible, the illustrations meant to sim-
plify thousands of years of cultural and religious iconography for an
eight-year-old. Art works beautifully as a tool of class. It can, even
from childhood, sow the seeds of identity conflict. Had I been born
elsewhere, elseway, would I imagine my faith as the kind of lineage
I see it as now? As a precious, shining rung on some heavenly ladder
rather than a rusty link in a chicken-wire fence?

"For me, irony is far too simplistic and expected," Vallance writes.
"To do the show seriously was the challenge . . . In this way I could infiltrate both sides." In practice, I also write with the desire to infiltrate.
But I do not want Vallance's vantage point. I want my own, which is
outside but inside at the same time. I want to channel whatever higher
power I see in The Highwaymen paintings, in Lauren Groff's Florida
stories, in the winsome chords of an early Jimmy Buffett record. I like
where I sit, even if I can't explain why. My faith is in this place itself,
its sacredness, something like a natural divinity. In resisting the urge
to be either fully critic or fully consumer when it comes to Florida,
in refusing to make it be either saintly or sinful, I think there is a
different kind of leverage.

The value, maybe, is in the ability to see things as they are. To look
clear-eyed at a fake bridge surrounded by plastic flowers in a concrete
room, to feel a thump on your back and a flashbulb in your face and
say confidently, however quietly, "This is not the landscape."

my god, rachel, how can you live here?

after Eve Babitz / City Magazine, 1975

When my sister and I were little girls, we were perpetually outside. We stayed with our grandparents in Jacksonville every summer, along with our boy-cousin Brice, who said my name like a number any time he was getting me in trouble: "R-eight-chul did it." On days when our energy was too much for the square footage of their double-wide, we would escape Brice's tyranny and walk down to the creek at the end of the dirt road, poking at its banks with old umbrellas and walking sticks. Our grandma's vegetable garden had weeds that needed pulling and grasshoppers that needed to be eradicated. She showed us how to pick them off of her rose bushes and pop their heads off between our thumb and index finger. Our still-pliable joints were put to use, shelling beans on their back porch before dinner. Her hands, my grandmother's, were paper-soft but still solid. Decades of tobacco picking and drying, the endless folding of dough into biscuits for a lifetime's worth of mornings, had worn on them like a lovely erosion, shaping them into cool alabaster that scrubbed my scalp in the bathtub or tickled my back until I fell asleep.

Back in Tampa, we could be found on most school nights riding bikes around a retention pond behind Robinson High School. Or, more accurately, my sister rode her bike—I was too scared to learn how—while I ran frantically alongside, gravel lodging itself between the plastic openings of my jelly shoes. We had always either just come from, or would soon be going, camping in one of the many state parks dotting the central corridor of Florida: Juniper Springs, Salt Springs, Rainbow River. We were always somewhere on the spectrum between soaking wet and wrung out and mildewy, but never completely dry from April to October. The specific body of water didn't matter—we were in it. Waist-deep in the sweet-tea water of some silty-bottomed lake, elbow-dropping each other in a neighbor's above-ground pool, or bumping up against manatees in an inner tube along the surface of the once-clear Ichetucknee River.

Every part of our bodies was burnt: the soles of our feet from hop-scotching across the molten asphalt that ran between the beach-access boardwalk and the car; above our belly buttons, where the absent-minded graze of a seatbelt buckle could make your skin bubble up and blister. Our skin would take on a viscosity that not even long showers could completely wash away, the sunscreen, bug spray, and sweat mixing together and baking into our nutbrown limbs like wood varnish. There was always a hot dog waiting for us at the end of an afternoon, in a bun made soggy from pruney fingertips. Our blood ran salty, diluted with gallons of lemon-lime Gatorade. The swelling TV static of cicadas lulled us to sleep, wrapped up like mummies in beach towels, nodding off in scratchy lawn chairs as the sun set and the grownups played cards on a picnic table well into the night.

To me, it was heaven. To be a child here, in the summer, is to not see the point of living anywhere else. We never wondered what people thought about our home. It never occurred to me to be ashamed of being from Florida.

~

My friends from New York or LA or Ames, Iowa, God bless them, often ask me the same question when they hear I've moved back to Florida: "How can you live there?" My first response is to ask them one right back: "Have you ever actually been to Florida?" They say that maybe they have, when they were a kid, once or twice. Their parents took them to Disney World, where they stayed in some sweaty-walled budget hotel outside of Kissimmee. "My great-aunt Ruth lives in Boca, and we go there in the spring." *Yeah, I bet,* I think, but do not say. Straight into a car at the Fort Lauderdale airport and then through the gates of an "active senior" community that doubles as a golf course. Poolside lunches and screened-in patios and manicured lawns. Straight back into the car and out across the highway a few days later, wiping her waxy goodbye-lipstick off their cheek with a grimace. They seem to think that is enough to make them an expert. They've had one sunburn; they've seen it all.

Or they tell me they took a girl's trip to Miami. Miami is the only place that people not from Florida seem to agree exists outside of our state's borders; Miami is its own universe. I would love to tell you about the mysteries of Miami, about Hialeah, Little Haiti, and Little Havana; the breezes in Coconut Grove; the matcha shops and fluorescent walls of Wynwood, the bronzed gladiators preening on the husk of what used to be South Beach. The octogenarian gargoyles of Aventura looming in the north, the final boss you must defeat before you leave paradise via I-95 and enter the shadow realm. But I have to stop there because I'm not from Miami; I'm from Florida.

Now that I've been living back here for a few years, my answer to that question—*How can you live there?*—changes. Or at least, I have to think about it a little bit longer. I'm not exactly embarrassed, but I'm not proud either. I've become a bit of a reluctant apologist for this place. People seem to like it when I write about growing up here, especially if they did too, but I don't think I want to anymore. I feel ashamed to be defending something that seems determined to destroy itself, to take everyone who lives here along with it. Every day, it feels more apparent that, although I do love Florida, Florida doesn't love me back.

I know why people don't want to live here. So do you. We saw the same election results, the horror on our faces reflected in the TV glow, but no shock. I'm not so blinded by my affection for the Florida of my past that I can't see the gore of its present.

Whenever Florida is in the news for something stupid, which is often, it happens. I wait for it to surface. Could probably set a stopwatch by it. Somewhere in my Twitter feed, usually, or in a group chat where people don't know me very well, they share memes and GIFs from TV shows like *30 Rock* or *Broad City* that use the state as a punchline. They talk about how people voted, as though that's a good reason why sixteen inches of seawater burst into their homes, ruined everything they own.

Having grown up in Florida, I've faced my fair share of shitstorms: environmental, political, and otherwise. What infuriates me is the futility. Why bother with the theatrics, the logistics, the sweat and tears? Florida has been abandoned, ideologically and culturally, for centuries. No one is coming to save us.

The heat alone is biblical, and the palmetto bugs feel like a personal hex. We have gigantic, invasive snakes. Sinkholes and "Stand Your Ground" and Casey Anthony. There is, of course, the unavoidable fact of our governor, a man with a heart like a hacksaw and terrible taste in protective footwear. Much as I'd love to talk about the lifts in his shoes and the abscesses in his soul, it's not worth it. He doesn't deserve levity. His policies actively endanger people I love, which makes it hard for me to joke. I see the compound effect of those kinds of jokes, after all, in the media and the memes and the mass exodus of Floridians to greener pastures. It's not hard for me to feel hopeless most of the time, given our state's track record. If there is one thing Floridians seem to agree upon, it is voting against their own interests.

But hopelessness isn't really the Floridian way, is it? The opposite is generally true. People who live in this place are notable precisely for their hopefulness, however cartoonishly misguided that hope may be. Take, for instance, their unwillingness to leave in the face of natural disasters. They believe the myths, that by coming here they might live forever, Juan Ponce de León's failures and the soaring heat index be damned. But I went to see the Fountain of Youth when I was in St. Augustine, hoping to find something that would make me feel like I hadn't wasted my own youth by having had the bad luck of being born here. I paid twenty bucks to walk through a tourist trap and prostrate myself before a pile of bricks, over which a rotten-egg smell lingered—the sulfuric spring water, trickling pathetically down into a grate marked with a plaque and its date of "discovery." A bedraggled peacock glared at me in the parking lot on my way out.

I'm having trouble being hopeful right now. The roof of Tropicana Field fluttered down First Avenue South in tatters after Hurricane Milton. Pieces of it sold on eBay for hundreds of dollars. I know someday I will walk into a bar owned by someone from Michigan and see a piece of my history mounted in a shadow box above a chalkboard advertising a sixteen-dollar margarita. If I sound reactionary, it's because I'm responding to the evidence mounting in front of me. My hope is calcifying into a gate around my heart. Historically, I have always stuck around for landfall, not wanting to abandon the ship. My fellow Floridians seem to think we will outlast every storm, but I don't know how much more water I can take on.

On the other hand, there is the beauty. Jimmy Buffett, God rest his sailor's soul, said as much in "The Weather Is Here, Wish You Were Beautiful." My friend Mara once attributed our difference of opinion on the state of Florida, existentially, to our similar difference of opinion on which bodies of water we found most appealing. Mara was living in Florida for grad school but was originally from New York State, where her beloved rivers run cold and clear over the smooth remnants of mountain rock. I myself am partial to the bathtub-warm waters of my Gulf of Mexico. I prefer my eroded rocks to be of the fine-grit, sugar-sand variety. The way Mara explained it was that people from Florida are just fundamentally different, that they care about things she might have a distant appreciation for, but would never truly grasp, not having grown up with them or only hearing about them secondhand.

I feel an ache in my bones when I am too far from the Gulf of Mexico. My mind feels landlocked, along with my body, if I am away for long stretches. I have tried to submerge them both into the Atlantic Ocean, all across the Eastern Seaboard, to test my theory about the Gulf's miraculous healing properties. I think it might just be me. I find that anywhere north of Jacksonville, the water grows too cold for my taste, the beach fronts too rocky, and all of the pleasures of the ocean that I am familiar with turn into obstacles to be overcome. I do not want to feel like a conqueror in the ocean, or even like I've met it as an equal. I want to acquiesce, to meld into it like I'm easing into a giant bathtub. I want to pee in the water and not be able to tell the difference in temperature. I love dragging the heels of my feet along its velvety floor, where flat fish with barbed tails lie in wait until I thunder nearby, that official state dance move of Florida, the stingray shuffle, announcing my presence.

My niece lives here, down the street from me, and one of the joyous possibilities of living here is that I might get to be there when she jumps off a causeway bridge for the first time. To see her launch herself into the sparkling green water of the Intracoastal and feel saltwater shoot up her nose as she hits the water, bracing for it with her small, strong arms at her sides. To watch as she comes up for air part laughing, part screaming, and remember the blood thumping in my head when I did it for the first time, the saltwater stinging my eyes. On long afternoons, when the sun is melting into cotton candy clouds, I get to watch her brother rise and sink above my vision as I sit criss-cross-applesauce on the trampoline while he jumps, shiny with sweat, his head bobbing the sun in and out of shadow like some knock-kneed angel.

I think I would be happy to sit on the sand of these beaches for the rest of my life, buy a metal detector, find and collect shells until my skin turns to leather. Living here means that on any given Monday, eleven months out of the year, I can be a human rotisserie chicken, achieve maximum crispiness in a few short turns, before I brine myself in saltwater again, over and over until the sun goes down. That's not nothing. Not to me.

And yet.

Some say that Florida is the canary in America's coal mine. I think that metaphor is a little too pretty. Those of us who love this place, despite all the evidence that we should not, are more like that ancient seagull you sometimes see on the beach and try to avoid. You know the one, with the crazy eyes, separated from the flock. Whenever we are in the news, it feels to me like we are screeching from the shore, with fucked-up feathers and a crooked wing, desperate for someone to help us, while tourists laugh and throw Hot Cheetos at us.

But they *are* here, those tourists, on our beaches. Despite their endless vitriol for this "godforsaken swamp," people from other parts of the country move here by the thousands every single day. They come from Duluth or Cleveland or Winnetka or wherever, looking for something they can't find anywhere else. They pack their orthopedic shoes and pickleball rackets and standing desks and move here without ever considering what it means to truly *live* here. They vote absentee, sending dutifully marked ballots off to their home states, sit on plastic-covered couches in their condos, and suck their teeth at our election results like disappointed schoolmarms. *That's Florida for you,* they say. They preach to the Facebook masses about our book bans and megachurches and open carry laws, but these things don't seem to discourage them from staying here, not when the golf course is calling and they don't have to pay income tax.

I feel sacred duty to be mean to them.

~

Many years ago, Eve Babitz was trying to answer the question I am trying to answer now, about her birthplace of LA. She says her more bohemian friends from San Francisco would say, "How can you live in LA, Eve, my God, *the architecture,*" to which she'd respond, "I love the architecture, but you have to know how to look; you cannot stay on the main drags or go on the freeway and see anything. You have to be willing to wander off, up in the hills (even the hills in the back of the Sunset Strip are pretty cute)." This is the only line of defense I can muster when it comes to explaining myself. I like looking. To be fair, there is a lot to look at, sometimes too much to take in at once.

There's this scene from the movie *The Last Black Man in San Francisco* that plays on repeat in my mind when I defend Florida. San Francisco, that once-bohemian bastion of culture where Eve Babitz's friends claim she should be residing instead of seedy, nasty, lowlife Los Angeles. Now, in this film, San Francisco has seen itself change in ways Eve's friends could not have imagined. In this scene, the main character, who is struggling to retain ownership of a family home in the face of gentrification, overhears two transplants on a bus talking about how much they hate San Francisco.

"The city is dead," one woman says.

He looks at them across the bus.

"You don't get to hate San Francisco," he says to her.

"I'll hate what I want," she says.

"But do you love it?" he asks her.

"I mean, yeah. I'm here."

He looks at her a minute and says, "You don't get to hate it unless you love it."

Eve Babitz says, "Maybe it's impossible for you San Franciscans, with your history all around you—the downtown, the proximity of the harbor, the rain and fog, the narrow houses, streets and driveways—it might be impossible for you to travel the short distance of only an hour and find yourself in wide-open placid spaces."

⁓

I'm still trying to land on a good answer, though, for my friends who aren't from here. When they step from the airport into the sadistic Florida sunlight, stagger under the humidity wrapped around them like a blanket, and they ask me, "My God, Rachel, how can you live here?" I just smile at them, usually. Valid question, one I could never answer in a way that would make them happy. I shrug or change the subject. If you don't know, I can't make you understand. You will keep

posting that Bugs Bunny GIF every election day, like clockwork, because it is easier to imagine centuries of humanity and history sinking
into the ocean and laugh than to hold multiple contradictory truths in
one's mind at the same time. I don't expect you to be able to do that if
you haven't seen the Florida I have seen, haven't watched it grow and
change and surprise and disappoint you, ad nauseam.

Before you ask me that question again, visitor, there are a few things
I need you to do.

Pass your great-aunt Ruth's and keep driving. Drive through
Homestead and see the people who grow and pick your groceries—
your strawberries, tomatoes, watermelons, cabbage, and sweet corn,
the sugarcane that sweetens your coffee. Stop at Robert Is Here and
bite into a guava so ripe it makes you cry. Come back up through
Plant City and save a few dollars. Stop at Dinosaur World, not Disney World. Smoke a joint at Roser Park in St. Pete and freak out a
little when the enormous, prehistoric sandhill cranes get close and
a splash to the east draws your attention to the sign that says, "DO
NOT MOLEST GATORS," and realize you are, right now, also inside
of dinosaur world.

Stop looking for a good bagel. There aren't any, and that's okay.
Instead, walk into the marbled, air-conditioned oasis of any Publix,
wind your way to the deli, and give yourself permission to order fried
chicken tenders on a fluffy white sub roll smothered in buffalo sauce,
assembled lovingly—if at a glacial pace—by a woman with a Betty
Boop tattoo. Grab a sweet tea, and maybe a sprinkle cookie, and find
the nearest beach to be alone with your spoils.

If you're feeling fancy, come in October, when stone crab season
starts. Go to the dimmest, stuffiest steakhouse you can find—we have
many. Give yourself over to the childlike glee you feel when the fixings
arrive at your white-clothed table, the gleaming silver crab crackers
and the tiny fork, the perfect half-moon of lemon encased in cheese-

cloth like a present. Marvel at the inky-black lacquered carapace of the claw, fading into a creamy coral. The armor of a creature that has evolved to regrow after they are broken, a perfect metaphor for us Floridians.

The most sustainable seafood on the planet, stone crab claws are not forced from their bodies, and their harvest does not cause the death of their owners. They are pulled up in nets, where a fisherman then applies pressure to the larger of their two limbs. There is a clicking sound, which is not a cracking off due to this pressure, but actually the crab itself releasing the claw of its own volition. Imagine, with solemnity, the zigzag walk of a she-crab who has done this over and over, cleaved herself in the face of a threat, given up the thing it has grown better and bigger each time in the name of self-preservation. Picture her lugging it around, that new claw, herky-jerky across the bottom of the ocean until the day she is pulled up, dripping, into the bright sun to do it all over again. Dunk the fruits of her resilience into melted butter, and be grateful for her example.

Other cities, maybe even your own, might be known for their strip clubs. But, oh baby, are ours special. On your journey, look for the establishments with deeply literary descriptors like Thee Dollhouse, Cheetah Lounge, the legendary Mons Venus. Have a few too many (you're on vacation!). If you keep your hands to yourself and your wallet open, you might be lucky enough to feel God on Dale Mabry Highway, as I have, in a VIP room shaped for no reason at all like a giant flying saucer. Afterward, celebrate your baptism with pancakes as big as your head at Three Coins, while the drunk couple next to you alternates between making out over the table and lovingly blowing clouds of vape smoke at one another.

Find the bookstore on First Avenue in St. Pete, a little place where people still go to spend their hard-earned money on beautiful stories. Peek into the back room of the store and see a desk, a half-dozen coffee cups crowding its surface, surrounded by lunch bags and bright mandarins and worn copies of well-loved books passed around among the people who work there like tokens of love. Watch every morning as they open their doors to hundreds of people who, headlines be damned, desperately want to read, who could give a shit about a book ban, and will tell you so loudly and proudly. Two women who are deeply in love run this place and came here because they saw that we needed it. The people who work there bring writers and poets and artists to share their passionate love of language, spreading a gospel of folding chairs and community, making their own little house of worship. Look closely at those bookshelves before you ask me about the scared little men who are afraid of their contents.

Go to Boyd Hill, to Fort De Soto, to the shell mounds of Cedar Key, and the shockingly blue springs scattered across the state like jewels. Go scalloping or noodling or, if you're brave and want to make a little extra cash, python hunting for a bounty in the Everglades. Skip Disney and go to a rodeo, the Strawberry Festival, the mullet toss in Homosassa. Watch mermaids twirl and blow bubbles at Weeki Wachee and get your palm read in Cassadaga. Visit Zora Neale Hurston's grave in Eatonville and remember that we have homegrown legends too, people who loved this place and preserved it forever in stories.

Once you have made this pilgrimage, you can ask me again how I can manage to live here. I wonder, though, if you will.

I love it here because I hate it too. I love it because someone has to. Many people already do, and they deserve champions and advocates and political allies and food banks and superintendents and trash men and mailwomen and good bartenders and EMTs who want them not to die. They deserve abortion access and gender-affirming care and the freedom to read books that show them the value of their own stories. One of the quickest ways to eradicate an entire group of people in the public imagination is to make them a punch line, to dismiss them. I often get the feeling that I was put on this particular patch of earth in order to say, "That joke is only funny when I tell it," even if that reduces me to the joke by association. I don't care if people think I am wrong, or corny, for still feeling hopeful about this place. I won't muzzle the part of me that thinks there is something left worth saving.

So, until people stop wearing Yankee jerseys to Rays games, I won't shut up. Until they stop forcing my friends out of their apartments, buying them up from underneath them so they can convert them into nautical-themed Airbnbs, I can't. Until the few people responsible for the thousands of book ban requests across this state pack up and cede ground, I will keep selling those books to unaccompanied minors. Until those who want our beaches but not our burdens stop chuckling or sneering and decide to actually *live* here, to do something, to join those of us who are trying to take on the immense responsibility of caretaking paradise, not just scavenging it, I will not stop being that fucked-up seagull, hobbling along the beach, squawking at anyone who might throw me something useful. I will never stop interrupting their existential sunbathing and shitting all over their hundred-dollar beach umbrellas as they try to ignore what has always been here.

The joke goes that real Floridians, to their own detriment and their credit, do not evacuate. When disaster is on the horizon, they buy handles of rum and an extra deck of cards. In the face of legislation that wants them dead, they extend their endless grace into action, into resistance, into full splits and death drops on stage at Enigma. They make their way through the blizzard of glitter and sweat and aerosol sunscreen that form a haze over Central Avenue at Pride in June; they walk into their overcrowded classrooms and wipe small noses and open books that tell the truth; they pour drinks and wash dishes and serve fried fish to vacationers. I can live here because they do too, those hundreds of thousands of people who choose to stay here with me, to keep looking for one another, to keep remembering what it was and imagining against all logical arguments what it still could be. They know what this place is worth, that it belongs to them too. If you're here right now, it is just as much yours to create as it is mine. Why does anyone love the place where they are from? Because it is theirs. This, the miles of coastline and swamp, is mine.

How could I live anywhere else?

acknowledgments

First and foremost, thank you to my parents, Verna Dee and Paul Knox, who raised me in the precious, beautiful, messy state of Florida. I love you so much. Mom, I am so grateful for your endless well of love, forgiveness, and dedication to our family. Your love of books, words, and education brought us here. Whenever people tell me I am brave, I know I get it from you, from following your example. Thank you for never settling. Dad, for loving me even when you didn't always understand me. I've done a lot of hard things, in part because you knew I could first (even if sometimes I still cry the whole time). I'm so grateful to both of you for taking all five of us camping and swimming and to the beach, for insisting that we appreciate our home and each other. I appreciate you for always trying your best to let me make my own choices and leading with love.

Thank you, Nickie, for being my first and very best friend and for fact-checking my version of events in real time for most of my life. Your fingerprints are all over this book. Thank you to my brothers Ben, Will, and Jack, and bonus brother Joey, for teaching me how to be a little less selfish and for bringing so much joy (and Meg and Madi, the best sisters) to our big, chaotic family. Thank you, Hudson and Virginia, for giving me hope for the future and for making me funnier. Thank you to Mike and Eileen and Jim and Fran for giving me Adam and for loving me. I'm so grateful for all of the extended family of Knoxes and Lynches who support me with so much loud, proud enthusiasm. I'm sorry if I may have embarrassed you on any of these pages, but knowing in my heart that you will love me no matter what I say is the reason I was able to write this book in the first place.

I'm forever indebted to everyone who read these essays in their early phases and helped make them better. Much of this book began at The New School, where the great and generous Alison Kinney changed my life by showing me what it meant to be in a writing community, for real. I am grateful every day that you took my writing seriously and convinced me to do the same. A big thanks to all of the amazing writers in that cohort, among them: Emelia Copeland Titus, Simone Allen, Alyson Zetta Williams, Morgan Lopez, Cortez, Syl, and Madeline, for your rigorous commitment to beauty and fun. Thank you to the 12th Street crew, especially Seth Graves, Aly Tadros, and Abby Zieve. I'm so lucky to have you as friends and writing inspiration. Thank you to Laura Cronk and Madge McKeithen for your writing instruction, encouragement, and for just being so damn *cool.*

I'm grateful to all of the writers and faculty at the University of South Florida, where this collection took its most cohesive shape. I owe a huge debt of gratitude especially to Julia Koets for your mentorship, guidance, and encouragement of this manuscript—and of me, as a person. Your support (and now friendship!) has meant so much to me. Thanks to Tom Hallock for encouraging my wild Emerson goose chase and loving this state through scholarship. Thanks to Andi Rinard and Destiny Howell for your camaraderie through the publishing process, for the venting sessions and juicy grad-school gossip, and for keeping me up to my ears in snacks. Thank you, Hal, for keeping me young at heart and inspiring me with your bravery. Thank you to my *90 Day Fiancée* writing partners, Jess Gallerie and

Rae Zalopany, for being my over-caffeinated cheerleaders and keeping me sane during a batshit crazy summer, two hurricanes, and dozens of bad writing weeks. You went to spin class for me! If that's not love, I don't know what is. You both kept me afloat during the home stretch of this book, and I can't thank you enough. Thank you to Mara Beneway for introducing all of us and for being my second favorite Rachel and my first favorite poet. All of you—your writing and friendship—are gifts I don't deserve.

To my Tombolo Books darlings—Alyssa, Amanda, Erin, Jackie, Kelsey, Mekhala, Nicole, and Ryan. I quite literally couldn't have done it without you, without all of the pep talks, coffees from next door, gossip sessions, '90s country playlists, covered shifts, trips to the Disco, Advil, hugs, tears, and endless snacks. Thanks for letting me yap your ears off instead of shelving sometimes. I know y'all are sick of me. To Alsace and Candice, you are the best bosses I've ever had. Sorry I wrote some of this on company time (I'm good for it!). Thanks for letting me be myself, for valuing me as I am, and for the second home you've given me. The bookstore is an oasis for so many, myself included. You made my life so much better. I love you all so much.

Thank you, Autumn and Audrey, my Florida girls, my succubi, my *butterfly, sugar babies.* You made me tougher, but you also cherished my softness, even while teasing me for it. *They're just jealous 'cause we're young and in love.* Thank you to Emma for decades of friendship, fighting, growing, free talk therapy, and for letting me get out my splinters both real and existential. Thank you, Devo, for keeping it so real it hurts sometimes and for always reminding me where I come from and where I can still go. Thank you, Brandon, for your endless love and laughter, for seeing me so clearly, and for being my shotgun rider 'til the day I die. Cassidy, thanks for being there for me through so many transformations and for being the funniest person I know. Lacey Ann, the Cantina girl of my dreams, the coolest person at every party, and luckiest of all, my friend. Thank you to Joey and Walker, my Statler and Waldorf in better outfits (and in love). I love you guys.

Credit is due to Fran Snyder, whose course "Words in Her Mouth: Women in Judaism, Christianity, and Islam" informed so much of "Deserter," and to the writer Annie Ernaux and her book *Happening,* without which I never would have found the courage to write it in the first place. They will probably never read this, but thank you to Sheila Heti, Durga Chew-Bose, Melissa Febos, Karen Russell, and Mary Karr for your books. I wouldn't be who I am without you. Thank you to Alicia Thompson, Tyler Gillespie, Gloria Munoz, and Roy Peter Clark for your advice and support, and to all the other St. Pete writers carving out space for literary community in my favorite place in the world.

Thank you to Jesse, Justin, and Zach at Tap House, where much of this book was written. You guys are the best, and the next round is on me. Thank you to Audrey and Brian Dingeman for being the best buds for so long, for hours spent distracted by baseball butts, letting me snuggle your dogs and swim in your pool when my brain was on fire, for sweaty hugs and belly laughs, and always being the first to check in during hard times. Thank you to Ryan Quinney for reading early drafts and always having a thoughtful new perspective I hadn't considered. Thank you to my New York Dolls: Sophie Christenberry, Monet Patterson, and Kelly Ann Sullivan. You were truly in the trenches of my twenties with me and accepted every version of myself, even when it meant I had to leave you to come back to this godforsaken swamp. The stupid breakups were the best thing that ever happened to me because I got you all. Thank you to Alix Caulk for understanding the Florida to New York to Florida pipeline more than anyone, and for making me love Tampa again because people like you are from there.

Thank you to Stephanye Hunter for her patience and enthusiasm, and for seeing a better version of this book than I had imagined. Your kindness means so much to me. Thank you to everyone at University Press of Florida for taking a chance on this project. Thank you to the marketing team, publishers, designers, and my wonderful copy editor Lyric Dodson for all of your help bringing this book into the world and to new readers. I'm in your debt.

And most importantly, to Adam. There aren't enough trees left on this planet to produce the amount of pages I would need to thoroughly express my gratitude and love. I am so, so lucky. Thank you for the years of unwavering support, loud confidence, and creative space you've given me. *Everything* I've been able to accomplish is because you first propped me up and cheered me on. I'm so glad you didn't change your number to a New York area code and that you didn't run away when I puked on your shoes early on. Thank you, most of all, for loving me. This book is your accomplishment as much as it is mine, and I hope I made you proud. As a great Florida man once said, "We ride together, we die together. Bad boys for life."

And to little Rachel: I am so proud of you for not giving up, for deciding to stick around. Thank you. See? It was all worth it.

references

Wild Things

McNaughton, John, director. *Wild Things*. Mandalay Entertainment, 1998.

O'Brien, Tim. *The Things They Carried*. Mariner Books Classics,
2009.

Harmange, Pauline. *I Hate Men*. Translated by Natasha Lehrer. 4th
Estate, 2022.

Spring Break Forever

Korine, Harmony, director. *Spring Breakers*. A24 Films, 2013.

Rockstar Games. 2023. "Grand Theft Auto VI Trailer 1" YouTube,
December 4, 2023. https://www.youtube.com/watch?v=
QdBZY2fkU-0.

Korine, Harmony, director. *The Beach Bum*. Neon, 2019.

Bowen, Peter. "The Little Rascals—Peter Bowen on Larry Clark's
Kids" *Filmmaker Magazine,* n.d. https://filmmakermagazine
.com/archives/issues/summer1995/rascals.php.

The Last Resort

Swanson, Jess. "Does Serial Killer Aileen Wuornos Haunt This Florida Dive Bar?" *Miami New Times,* October 26, 2021. https://www.miaminewtimes.com/news/does-the-ghost-of-aileen-wuornos-haunt-this-florida-dive-bar-13196021.

Wuornos v. State, Supreme Court of Florida, September 22, 1994.

Travis, Randy. "Diggin' Up Bones," recorded 1985, track 4 on *Storms of Life,* Warner Records.

Berry-Dee, Christopher, and Aileen Wuornos. *Monster: My True Story.* John Blake Publishing Ltd, 2006.

Jenkins, Patty, director. *Monster.* Newmarket Films, 2003.

Haynes, Todd, director. *May December.* Netflix, 2023.

Zuniga, Joe. *A Crown of Beauty for Ashes: A biography of the life of Debra Jean Beasley.* Peppertree Press, 2016.

"Debra Lafave, Teacher Convicted of Sex with Student, Ordered Back on Probation." *Tampa Bay Times,* August 15, 2012. https://www.tampabay.com/news/courts/debra-lafave-teacher-convicted-of-sex-with-student-ordered-back-on/1245978/.

"It Is a Queer Place"

Emerson, Ralph Waldo, Edward Waldo Emerson, and Waldo Emerson Forbes. *Journals of Ralph Waldo Emerson with annotations.* vol. VI, 1841–1844. Houghton Mifflin; The Riverside Press, 1911.

Emerson, Ralph Waldo (1939) "Emerson's Little Journal at St. Augustine, January, February, March, 1827," *Florida Historical Quarterly* Vol. 18: No. 2, Article 4.

A Florida Enchantment. United States, United States: General Film Co., Library of Congress, Smithsonian Institution, distributed exclusively by Image Entertainment, 1914.

Emerson, Ralph Waldo, and Merton M. Sealts. *The Journals and Miscellaneous Notebooks of Ralph Waldo Emerson. Volume V, 1835–1838.* Belknap Press of Harvard University Press, 1965.

Stein, Jordan Alexander. "History's Dick Jokes: On Melville and Hawthorne." *Los Angeles Review of Books,* December 15, 2015. https://lareviewofbooks.org/article/historys-dick-jokes-on -melville-and-hawthorne/.

"'CINCINNATI FACTOR' VS. FLORIDA IDENTITY." *Orlando Sentinel,* August 3, 2021. https://www.orlandosentinel.com/1993 /05/02/cincinnati-factor-vs-florida-identity/.

Agua Mala

Amann, David. "Agua Mala." *The X-Files* Season 6, Episode 13. Fox, February 21, 1999.

Delva, Shernide. "Delray Beach Firefighters Combat Overdoses; Narcan Not Always Enough." *Palm Partners,* November 18, 2016. https://www.palmpartners.com/delray-beach-sees-record -breaking-88-overdoses-in-october/.

Del Pozo, Brandon, Josiah D. Rich, and Jennifer J. Carroll. "Police Reports of Accidental Fentanyl Overdose in the Field: Correcting a Culture-Bound Syndrome That Harms Us All." *The International Journal on Drug Policy,* November 2021. https://pmc .ncbi.nlm.nih.gov/articles/PMC8810663/#R3.

Smith, Jane. "Along the Coast: Chiefs Express Concern for First Responders' Mental Health." *The Coastal Star,* September 29, 2016. https://thecoastalstar.com/profiles/blogs/delray-beach -chiefs-express-concern-for-first-responders-mental-h.

"Facts about Fentanyl." DEA. Accessed November 8, 2024. https://www.dea.gov/resources/facts-about-fentanyl.

"Pinellas County Opioid Task Force Strategic Plan 2020–2022."

Pinellas County, Florida: Opioid Strategic Planning Committee, 2020.

Segal, David. "In Pursuit of Liquid Gold." *New York Times,* December 27, 2017. https://www.nytimes.com/interactive/2017/12/27/business/urine-test-cost.html.

Deserter

Trible, Phyllis. *Texts of Terror: Literary-Feminist Readings of Biblical Narratives.* Fortress Press, 2022.

Genesis 16:7 (New International Version).

Kendall, Jackie, and Debby Jones. *Lady in Waiting: Becoming God's Best While Waiting for Mr. Right.* Destiny Image, Inc, 2014.

Heti, Sheila. *Motherhood.* Henry Holt and Company, 2019.

Kordova, Shoshana. "Word of the Day Akeret Bayit: Barren or Bedrock Woman?" *Haaretz,* November 10, 2013. https://www.haaretz.com/2013-11-10/ty-article/.premium/word-of-the-day-akeret-bayit-a-homey-term/0000017f-dc6e-d3a5-af7f-feeeabf50000.

Motel Art

Kuskey, G. Eric, and Bettina Gilois. *Billion Dollar Painter: The Triumph and Tragedy of Thomas Kinkade, Painter of Light.* Weinstein Books, 2014.

Boylan, Alexis L. *Thomas Kinkade: The Artist in the Mall.* Duke University Press, 2011.

Vallance, Jeffrey. "'Thomas Kinkade's Heaven on Earth.'" Essay. In *Thomas Kinkade: The Artist in the Mall.* Duke University Press, 2011.

"Thomas Kinkade: 'Heaven on Earth,' curated by Jeffrey Vallance.

Part 1 of 2." YouTube, August 31, 2010. https://www.youtube
.com/watch?v=64moi6a8wPY.

Didion, Joan. *Where I Was From.* Vintage International, 2011.

Derr, Mark. "ARTS IN AMERICA; Sunshine for Windy Dream-
scapes." *New York Times,* November 27, 2001. https://www
.nytimes.com/2001/11/27/books/arts-in-america-sunshine-for
-windy-dreamscapes.html.

My God, Rachel, How Can You Live Here?

Babitz, Eve. *I Used to Be Charming.* The New York Review of Books,
Inc, 2019.

Talbot, Joe, director. *The Last Black Man in San Francisco.* A24
Films, 2019.

Rachel Knox is a writer and bookseller born and raised in Tampa Bay. She holds a BA from the Riggio Honors Writing Program at The New School in Manhattan and an MFA in creative writing from the University of South Florida. She lives in St. Petersburg, Florida.